# Augustine of C

The shrine of St Augustine at Canterbury

*See note p. 59*

# Augustine of Canterbury

## by

## Margaret Deanesly
Late Professor Emeritus, University of London, D. Litt. Lambeth.

The Saint Austin Press
Southampton
1997

The Saint Austin Press
PO Box 610
Southampton
SO14 0YY

First published 1964 by Thomas Nelson.

© The literary estate of the late Margaret Deanesly,
The Church of the Annunciation, Bryanston Street, London W1.

© 1997, This edition, The Saint Austin Press, Southampton.

A catalogue record for this book is available from the British Library

Printed in Great Britain by BPC Wheatons, Exeter.

† Published to celebrate the 1400th anniversary of the landing in England of Saint Augustine of Canterbury. A.M.D.G.

*"O God, who by the preaching and miracles of Thy confessor and bishop, blessed Augustine, didst vouchsafe to enlighten the English nation with the light of the true faith; moved by his prayers, vouchsafe that the hearts of those who have gone astray may return to the unity of Thy truth, and that we may ever be of one mind in doing Thy will. Through our Lord Jesus Christ Thy Son, who liveth and reigneth with Thee and the Holy Ghost, God for ever and ever. Amen"*

*Collect for the Feast of Saint Augustine of Canterbury.*

# Preface

IN any account of the work of Augustine of Canterbury little can be added to what Bede tells us, so unforgettably, of the inception and course of his mission to the English. I have merely tried to explain for modern readers the kind of man Augustine was; to show the Roman world he came from, the Cantware people to whom he came, and the gradual revolution his coming brought. Augustine, since the Reformation, has had on the whole 'a bad press', especially as contrasted with that of the Celtic saints, with their freshness and simplicity. His grave and accomplished Latin mind was much in contrast with theirs; yet the work he did was fundamental. He brought Christianity to the English: he was the instrument of Pope Gregory, the founding father of the English Church.

I should apologise for one transgression beyond the borders of history. Livy supplied the speeches of his generals before their battles and nobody is disturbed by that: I have supplied a few words to Augustine and the interpreter and Æthelberht, words suggested by the writings of Gregory or Anglo-Saxon sources, and I hope this will not disturb anyone either.

I have dealt with the subject of the Rule of the Master and the Rule of St Benedict at some length in Appendix I, because the minsters founded by Augustine and his followers all followed the old, unwritten tradition of the monastic life, and on this old *vita monachica* the Rule of the Master throws as much light as that of the better known Rule of St Benedict.

For ease of reading Anglo-Saxon proper names and other words are in this book spelt in normal characters, without symbols or accents. I follow Sir Frank Stenton's spelling in *Anglo-Saxon England*.

I owe thanks for help to many scholars, among whom I should mention specially Dom John Stéphan, O.S.B., of Buckfast Abbey, and Professor Sheppard S. Frere, to whom I owe much enlightenment about late Roman Canterbury and the wooden buildings of the Cantware, as Augustine found them and to Professor F. Wormald.

MARGARET DEANESLY

v

# Contents

| | | |
|---|---|---|
| 1 | St Augustine's Background and Training | I |
| 2 | The Sending of the Mission to England | 23 |
| 3 | The Sending of Fresh Helpers in 601 | 44 |
| 4 | Augustine's Queries and Gregory's Answers | 60 |
| 5 | Augustine and the 'Bishops of Britain' | 76 |
| 6 | What Augustine Brought to Britain | 89 |
| 7 | The Sequel to Augustine's Work | 108 |
| 8 | The *Vita Monachica* in England after Augustine | 128 |
| | Appendix I: The Rule of the Master (RM) and the Rule of St Benedict (RSB) | 134 |
| | Appendix II: The early form of the vigil and divine office and the relation of the Roman-basilican office to the Benedictine rule | 151 |
| | Bibliography | 158 |
| | Index | 160 |

## CHAPTER I

# St Augustine's Background and Training

ST AUGUSTINE is reverenced in the English Church as the missionary who brought Christianity to southern England and founded the metropolitan see of Canterbury. On the gospel book he used at the altar, sent to him by Pope Gregory the Great, archbishops of Canterbury have taken and still take their corporal oath to protect the rights and liberties of 'this Cathedral and Metropolitical Church of Christ, Canterbury'. The offering of this age-old manuscript by the dean to the new archbishop, about to take possession of his see, is the most moving part of the enthronement ceremony. Whatever estimate is held of Augustine's work, it is undeniable that he founded the church of Canterbury and the Anglo-Saxon episcopate.

He brought the Christian religion to the pagan Anglo-Saxons of south-east Britain; and, with the religion, contact with the old civilisation of the Mediterranean. The Anglo-Saxons were not uncivilised: they had come a long way from primitive tribalism, and a very long way from using the earliest art-forms towards expressing the human appreciation of beauty in gold and silver work; but they had never had contact themselves with the far older cultures of Greece and Rome.

From the survivors of the Romano-Britons whom they had conquered they had learned little. They had their (oral) laws: they were passing from the old punishment of homicide by the blood feud to the newer, more humane, punishment by payment of graded fines by the murderer's kin; but there was a great difference between enforcing order by wers and wites and bots and the subtleties of Roman law, as known to their new Italian teachers. Indeed, there was as great a difference as that between the old, bloody religion of Thor and Woden and the new cult of Christ the victor, who triumphed on

Easter Day over death and the old war gods. Augustine brought the over-king, the *bretwalda* Æthelberht, a new religion; and he reopened the channels of communication with the old, Greco-Roman civilisation of the Mediterranean.

For an account of the sending of Augustine by Pope Gregory I in 596 we have, ever since the days of Bede, relied upon the account he gave in his *Ecclesiastical History of the English People*. He finished it in A.D. 731. It was a very good account, for Bede was a very fine historian, and he was in touch with contemporary scholars in Canterbury, who handed on to him all that they knew of the traditions of that church, and also copies of the letters sent by Pope Gregory and other early popes to Augustine and his successors. Bede's history was recognised as a monument of scholarship from his own day onwards: English bishops and abbots studied it, Alfred the Great had it turned into the English of Wessex, and a king of Mercia tried to make political use of it in an effort to have the southern archbishopric transferred to a city within the boundaries of his own kingdom. Through Bede, all men knew that Augustine slept at Canterbury and how he came to sleep there; and to Bede's story of his mission and its results not very much can be added. Archaeologists, art historians and numismatists, however, have added to our knowledge of what English society was like in Augustine's day, and continental historians to our knowledge of the Roman monastery from which he came. For the actual history of the earliest church at Canterbury we still rely on Bede.

In one respect, however, historical research in the last thirty years has made a very great difference to what was believed about Augustine's mission: namely, to what was meant by Bede's assertion that Augustine was a monk, which was long thought to imply that he introduced a 'Benedictine' kind of monachism into England. Bede lived long before Charles the Great and his counsellor, Benedict of Aniane, laid down in the Council of Aix, 817, that all monks should follow the Benedictine rule and, in consequence, Bede never called Augustine a 'Benedictine' monk. But later scholars and writers, right down to this century, took for granted the Carolingian direction that monks should be Benedictine, and assumed that monks had been Benedictine ever since Pope

Gregory the Great devoted a whole book in his *Dialogues* to extolling the life, miracles and wise monastic rule of the great abbot of Monte Cassino. It was assumed that since Gregory so much admired the Benedictine rule, it would have had a magisterium in the monastery he himself founded *ad clivum Scauri* [1] and dedicated to St Andrew; and that Augustine, trained in this monastery, must, therefore, have been in some sense a Benedictine monk.

The work of Italian scholars on the early monasteries at Rome, and that of many Benedictine and other scholars on the Benedictine rule, its sources, and other rules of the sixth and seventh centuries, have much modified our knowledge of the kind of monasticism practised in Rome in the days of St Benedict and of Pope Gregory; it was not Benedictine in the modern sense, where, as at Downside or Solesme or Montserrat today, all the monks profess to follow the Benedictine rule. The *regula* which the monks of Gregory's monastery *ad clivum Scauri* obeyed was the *regula* of their abbot, the daily monastic observance and custom which he maintained, as best suited to his own monastery. Obedience to the *regula* was implied in the monk's profession of obedience to the abbot. As abbot he had been chosen or appointed as one well-versed in the 'norm of the monastic life', and he had to guide him certain old monastic rules to which great reverence was accorded. But the detailed form in which the monastic life was followed in his abbey was, in fact, his own.

This fresh light on the kind of monasticism in which Augustine had been trained illuminates the history of Augustine's mission and the early Church of the Anglo-Saxons. It affects the question whether the church of the Saviour at Canterbury was served by 'monks', or (as some have suggested) by 'canons'. It affects our view of what the episcopal *familiae* of the other early cathedral churches were. It affects the whole question of the early minsters in Anglo-Saxon England. It explains the kind of monastery that Augustine desired to establish under the patronage of SS Peter and Paul in his own see city. It renders no longer obscure the request of Benedict Biscop (and note his name, Benedict, taken, apparently, on

---

[1] The hill where Gregory founded his monastery in his paternal villa; the contemporary name for the monastery of St Andrew

entrance to the monastic life), that his monks should duly
observe the seventeen monastic rules which he had collected
for them. It illuminates the whole history of the training of the
clergy, the whole history of the conversion of England in the
south.

The devotion of some space to the modern view of
Augustine's background in Rome, then, scarcely needs any
apology: some knowledge of it is necessary for the appreciation
of his work in Kent. Augustine was a monk, even though, as
soon as he was consecrated bishop, he was automatically transferred (in sixth-century terms) from the monastic to the
clerical servitude and released from his obligations as a monk.
Pope Gregory I, who sent him to Britain, chose to send a monk,
the leader of a band of monks, deliberately: Augustine was
monk and abbot when he arrived in Britain.

Gregory chose to send him, though there were plenty of
secular clergy in Rome and plenty of devout laymen; Gregory
knew the possibilities well. He himself had been trained as a
monk, though he had been taken out of his monastery and made
papal deacon in 578 (these papal deacons managed all the
administrative affairs of the Roman see). It is true that he was
sent as *apocrysarius* (the Greek for secretary) to Constantinople
shortly after; but he was back in Rome in 587, signing documents as deacon to the apostolic see: one such document has
survived. He was again immersed in Roman business. He
ruled the Roman church from A.D. 590 to A.D. 604 as pope,
and at a time of great danger from the Lombard invasions. He
knew the crowds of refugee monks and clergy; he knew the
personnel of the great Roman basilicas and the many smaller
churches. Yet from all these he selected for the apostolic work
of the conversion of the English a band of Roman monks.
They were certainly not mission preachers, though Augustine
himself must have been selected as capable of episcopacy and,
therefore, of the apostolic work of preaching; they had been
trained as monks, regarding it as part of the monastic life to
remain within the monastery, except when sent on some
errand for the good of the monastery by the abbot. As monks,
they could not baptise or say mass—or not till they were given
holy orders by a bishop. They had had, emphatically, a

monastic training; yet they were chosen, rather than a band of
secular clergy, for the mission. Why?

Because they had dedicated their lives to God in a peculiar
way as the 'slaves of God' (*servi dei*). They were trained in
obedience and prayer; they would go to darkest England, not
knowing a word of English, hearing by rumour that this was a
very perilous mission, from which they would certainly never
return, and where death was likely to be unpleasant. A Gallo-
Roman carving, much earlier of course than Gregory's day,
shows a human victim hanging head downwards by his feet,
with his head extended and his throat bare, so that his throat
might be cut and the blood flow into the bucket placed ready
beneath. Not very nice. It is not surprising that the Roman
clergy, in holy orders and minor orders, did not overwhelm
Pope Gregory with offers to go to the barbarous lands of the
English; at any rate, not until after the mission was well
established and under the protection of the king.

Not only was the mission dangerous, but the Roman clergy
might well think that these were very dangerous days in Rome
herself, with the city full of refugees, and the savage Lombards
hammering, in 593, at the gates. This was hardly the time for
a great mission to the English? It is extraordinary indeed that
Pope Gregory persevered in sending it, but not that he sent
monks. It is more than possible that he had no choice.

There was, of course, a certain relation between monks and
secular clergy at the time, in that they both had the tonsure
and were by profession dedicated to the service of God. The
Greek word *kleros*, 'lot', lies behind the word 'clergy', and
those who had received the tonsure from bishop or abbot,
as a sign of their dedication, had recited with him the verse
from the Psalms: 'The lot is fallen unto me in a fair ground:
yea, I have a goodly heritage.' They had the *kleros*. But while
those who received the tonsure from the bishop would go on,
it was hoped, to pastoral work, for which education and at least
literacy was required, those who received the monastic tonsure
were dedicated to God's service in prayer and the practice of a
communal, ascetic life; there might be scholarly monks, but
scholarship and even literacy were not necessary. The clerical
order was conceived of in Augustine's time as separate from
the monastic order; if a monk were transferred from his

monastery to the service of the bishop, he was freed from his monastic obligations. Such an expression as 'the monastic clergy' was, however, appropriate, because both secular clergy and monks had the tonsure. The life for which they had been trained differed; yet Gregory regarded well-trained monks as good missionary material.

About the monasticism, then, that had trained both Pope Gregory and the monks he sent to England: some understanding of its nature is needed, because without it the nature of the life in the English minsters cannot be appreciated. Augustine converted the *bretwalda*, he founded the English episcopate in southern Britain, and he left behind him the minster as the agent for the conversion of England and the sole maintenance of pastoral life for about a hundred and fifty years, and one of its supporters for much longer. The minsters early and late served as training grounds for bishops who advised the king in folk moot and witan; they were very important agents in the conversion of the country and the passing over of the Mediterranean tradition to the Anglo-Saxons. The remainder of this chapter attempts, therefore, to deal with the stage which monastic development had reached in the Mediterranean countries when Augustine was sent to Britain. A good deal of space is devoted to the old Rule of the Master, because some of its detail illustrates the old, unwritten, traditional concept of the monastic life, the *vita monachica*, better than the Rule of St Benedict. The Rule of the Master was much longer than the Rule of St Benedict. The relationship of the two rules has been recently much discussed, and is important for an appreciation of Augustine's background and his work in England.

The *vita monachica* in Augustine's day was a much earlier form of monasticism than that suggested to most people by the words monk, monastery, abbot and the like. It did not at all resemble life in the great medieval abbeys like those of Winchester, Peterborough or St Albans. There was nothing feudal about it—nothing of the abbey owing knight-service to the king; the abbot as lord of great landed estates and with his own law-court were far in the future. So were the liturgical splendours, the delicate beauty of plain chant, all the reverent delight in words and music which Cluny added to the monastic recitation of the office; Cluny itself was more than three hundred years ahead. Whatever Augustine and the monks did in St Andrew's monastery *ad clivum Scauri* and later at Canterbury, it was nothing like that.

Monastic life in Italy in the sixth century, in the days of Benedict and his predecessors, was supported by a great tradition, the tradition of how a man should take a straight course to God according to the teaching of the desert Fathers. In its early form, it was a solitary life, and so little was it then a monk's duty to attend at any communal ritual or liturgy, that a monk's stealing off to attend the night praises and eucharist of the bishop and his clergy brought only reproof from the old monk who guided his soul. The solitary monk, fighting the lonely battle of the desert, prayed the psalms and read the divine scriptures by himself, and when Pachomius (c. 290–346) gathered monks into a community in Egypt, and they began to recite the night prayers together, there was still no common day-time timetable of office, meals and work. A monk was not bound to follow the meal timetable: he might prolong his fast as long as his individual endurance could sustain it.

It was the Greek monks, under their teacher, St Basil, who built up the communal side of the monastic life, with the communal recitation of the divine office as its framework. When Egyptian monasticism spread to the western, Latin, end of the Mediterranean, with Cassian, the Latin counterpart of Basil, monastic life was already communal, coenobitic, with a common timetable both for day and night. But even so, though the office was recited in the oratory, or oratories, by all, and on a note (for the ordinary spoken voice does not carry across a large room), it was, by modern standards, brief and plain; or, if prolonged, prolonged by the number of psalms sung or lessons read, and not by ceremonial action or sung melodies. It was the bishop's clergy, his deacons and lectors, who developed the use of the chant, and this at the eucharist, singing the introit and gradual psalms and the alleluia. Monasticism, in Benedict's and Gregory's day, was on its way to being what continental scholars call 'ritualised': the monk's day and night were subdivided by the offices, but 'ritualisation' implied no elaborate ceremonial or singing.

The essence of the monastic life was, as in the desert, the

complete withdrawal (*ascesis*) from life in the world in order
that the monk might attend to God. It was entered upon by the
postulant's prayer for admission ('Let not an easy entrance,'
said St Benedict, 'be granted him'); by the new brother's
renouncing all use of his goods and property and living the
common life under obedience to the abbot. This only took
place after a period of probation, during which all the hardships
of the life were explained to him, the period perhaps lasting
anything up to three years. The new brother then solemnly, in
the presence of the congregation, promised to follow the
monastic manner of life (*conversatio morum*), renounced his
property and promised obedience to the abbot. To St Benedict,
at Monte Cassino, he also promised 'stability' (*stabilitas*), to
remain in that monastery till death.

Thereafter he would recite the office with the brethren in the
oratory, attend the eucharist if it were Sunday or a feast day and
if one of the brethren were a priest, be directed to such work
under a senior as was enjoined by the abbot, and have the main
meal earlier or later according as it was a *feria* or a fast day. The
timetable differed in the winter and summer seasons, and the
fasting under the Lenten timetable was severe. A monastery
was not a *diaconia* such as the Greek monks had introduced into
Rome, expressly for the feeding of the poor and refugees; but
the poor might ask alms at the gate of the monastery, and would
receive such food and shelter as the monks could give them. All
this might be described as in the general monastic tradition.

There were many monasteries in Italy, Gaul and even Spain,
before Benedict founded Monte Cassino, and it is unlikely that
all abbots wrote a précis of the manner of life in their monasteries; knowledge of the rules of Pachomius, Basil and Cassian,
together with a general apprehension of the principles of
monastic life as practised by the desert Fathers, sufficed them.
When Pope Gregory I founded his monastery at Rome, the
monastery in which Augustine was trained as monk and rose to
the position of *praepositus*, this tradition of the monastic life was
fundamental. Gregory had great resources which he used for
the endowment of his house; he selected a good abbot, a refugee
monk, to be head of the house he himself entered as postulant.
It is scarcely to be doubted also that he would have secured for
the new monastery the necessary minimum of scriptures, choir

books and rules on the monastic life. The latter would be for
the guidance of the abbot, who would establish a daily timetable and rule of discipline.

There has been much discussion in recent years about two
issues affecting the house in which Augustine was trained: the
question whether two important written rules were known to
the abbots of Gregory's monastery *ad clivum Scauri* in Rome,
to Pope Gregory and to Augustine, and the question of the relation of these rules to each other.[1] It is now held that the old
Rule of the Master (the RM)[2] was anterior to the Rule of Saint
Benedict (the RSB),[3] and it is also held that the RSB was known
to Pope Gregory and his monastery, and therefore presumably
to Augustine. It is not held that the RSB was the exclusive rule
of the house. (For the question of the provenance of the RM

[1] The course of this controversy is well summarised in 'La controverse
Regula Magistri-Regula Sancti Benedicti (à propos d'un livre récent)' by
E. Manning in *Collect. Ord. Cisterc. Ref.* (1962, no. 2), 159–68. The anteriority of
the RM was first argued by Dom Alamo in *Rev. d'hist. Eccl.* XXXIV (1938),
739–53, and directly claimed by P. Genestout in *Rev. d'Ascétique et de Mystique*
(1940), 51–112; and, after the war, in the *Studia Anselmiana* (1947), 227–72.
Later, the struggle about the RSB was maintained by two eminent Benedictine
scholars. Dom O. Porcel, O.S.B., a monk of Montserrat, published in 1950 *La
doctrina monastica de san Gregorio Magno y la 'regula monachorum'*, and this
work was fiercely attacked by Dom K. Hallinger, of the Anselmian College in
Rome, a professor at the Vatican university; he provided a most useful study of
the 'mixed rule', but would not allow that Pope Gregory had even seen the
Benedictine rule; Pope Gregory belonged, not to the disciples of Benedict, but
to the school of Abbot Equitius (d. 571) of Valeria; he claimed, also, that Pope
Gregory's relation to St Benedict must be reviewed in the light of his own
writings and of contemporary evidence, rather than that of Carolingian historians. In 1960 Dom Porcel replied to Dom Hallinger's attack, in his *San
Gregorio Magno el Monacato,* in which he used only contemporary evidence
and claimed to prove that Pope Gregory indeed knew the RSB and was guided
by it, though not, of course, in his correspondence insisting that monasteries in
a quite different tradition should accept the detailed directions of the RSB. The
reviewer of this book in the *Collect. Ord. Cisterc. Ref.* (1962, no. 3) accepts the
view of Dom Porcel that the RSB was known in Gregory's monastery, and by
Gregory, as against that of Dom Hallinger, that it was not. Dom Porcel's view
has been generally accepted.
[2] Published as vol. III of *Scriptorium* publications by H. Vanderhofen,
F. Masai and P. B. Corbett, *La règle du Maître,* 1953 (édition diplomatique), with
discussion of the origin of the MSS edited and the contents of the rule. For the
order of office in the RM see Dom A. de Vogüé in 'Règle du Maître' in *Rev.
Bénéd.* LXX (1960), 410–13.
[3] See for the text C. Butler, *Sancti Benedicti Regula Monasteriorum,* 1935,
and, for a good modern translation and commentary, Dom A. Dumas, O.S.B.,
*La règle de saint Benoit, Paris,* 1961, as showing how far St Benedict followed
monastic tradition, and where his provisions were novel. Dom Dumas accepts
the anteriority of the RM as more than probable.

and its relation to the RSB, and for the evidence as to how much knowledge of St Benedict and his rule was available to Pope Gregory, see Appendix I.)

There were many monasteries in Rome [1] when Gregory, and later, Augustine, felt the call to the monastic life; and, indeed, other forms of the dedicated Christian life were open to them.

Both men would have been familiar with the basilica of St Peter on the Vatican mount, the holiest place in the city, and with the clergy who served it. The basilica had been built at Constantine's order over the cemetery adjoining the gardens where St Peter had suffered; it was built on an inconvenient, sloping site for no other reason than that the architects believed it was the burial place of St Peter. The building was focused on the holy spot where the marble shrine, the *aediculum*, covered the portion of wall, with its two niches, which was believed to mark the spot where St Peter's body rested after his martyrdom. Gregory and Augustine would have known too the basilica on the road to Ostia, where St Paul lay. They would have known the monks of the two small monasteries beside St Peter's (see p. 155).

They knew too the great basilica of the Saviour, beside the old Lateran palace, where the bishop of Rome had his *cathedra*, his chair, and where his *familia* said the old episcopal offices from vespers till the dawn office and the mass. The clergy of the *familia* were undergoing the very long training for the diaconate and priesthood, and they assisted the pope in his pastoral charge. They were not monks and had much work to do: they did not say any day offices between mass and vespers; such offices were sustained by the monks of the two basilican monasteries of St Stephen and St Pancras. They would know the old basilica of St Mary ad Praesepem, with its small attendant monastery, and the churches without the walls, such as the catacomb church beside the resting-place of the martyr Sebastian, which also had a choir of monks.

They would know the *diaconiae*, the service monasteries introduced by the Greeks, on which the early popes bestowed alms, and later ones took over as the official almshouses for the

---

[1] See plate i of Ferrari's *Early Roman Monasteries*, which has also plans of the Lateran basilica with its attendant monasteries, and the basilican monasteries of the Vatican, S. Mariae Maioris, St Paul on the road to Ostia, etc.

feeding of the poor. They would know of the Greek refugee monks, who had fled from one imperial heresy-hunt or other at Constantinople, and who served the *diaconiae*.

But Gregory desired the *conversatio monastica* in a monastery of the Latin tradition, and this too was possible in Rome. 'No other city in Christendom, save perhaps Constantinople, witnessed the flowering of monastic life as did Rome.' Compared with flourishing monasteries like Bobbio or Lérins, or with those early foundations in the east where monks could be reckoned in decades, most of these Roman monasteries in Gregory's day were small. They fell into three categories: the *diaconiae*, the monasteries attached to a basilica with the purpose of providing a choir office, and the monasteries founded for no other reason than that men and women might lead the *vita monachica* in the tradition of the desert Fathers. These were the most numerous.

To none of the Roman monasteries did Gregory feel himself called. He gave up his family possessions and with them founded six new monasteries in Sicily; with his family home and other estates not too distant he founded a great monastery *ad clivum Scauri*. It was clearly his intention to found a great house in Rome itself, a place as safe as any in Italy from the ravages of the invading Lombards, and to fill it with refugee monks who had escaped before them. To have joined a basilican monastery would have been to undertake monastic life with a special slant, the assiduous attendance at a great church thronged with pilgrims, and one step farther from the desert than the great house monasteries of the countryside. To turn his paternal villa into a monastery, one that would hold many monks, was to create a setting like that implied in the villa-monastery of the old RM; it would make a very good desert in the heart of Rome. Gregory entered as a postulant.

Recent research has established the number and situation of the monasteries in Rome in Gregory's day, the Rome with which 'the monk from my monastery, Augustine', was also familiar. Monasticism in the city has some bearing on Augustine's dispositions when he was established in his apostolic work at Canterbury. Though in Rome monks had as yet no pastoral charge, they were already sustaining the recitation of the divine office in the great basilicas, not merely by night, but by day; these Roman basilican monasteries, with which Gregory and Augustine were familiar, offer an apparent pattern for the celebration of mass and office at Christ Church, Canterbury, later (see p. 155). The early bishop and his clergy had, for the feasts and Sundays, celebrated an office that began at vespers (followed in very early days by the agape), and continued with a vigil service that ended with the dawn office and the eucharist; there were no day offices. It was not till small monasteries had begun to spring up all over the west, where monks said the canonical hours by day as well as by night, that popes and bishops began to found special small monasteries beside their great basilicas, that monks might chant the day hours (particularly) and the night hours. With crowds of pilgrims resorting to the shrine where the martyr or the holy founder of the church lay, it seemed right to the popes that prayers before the shrine should be offered 'continually', or in the offices which had resulted from the desert monks' efforts to 'pray continually'.

Roman monasteries were then, in Gregory's day, numerous. There were the fifth-century monasteries 'In Catacumbas', the first founded expressly that monks might say the divine office where the body of a martyr or martyrs had rested; 'Ad Lunam', a house perhaps named from a site marked by a piece of classical sculpture or stone carving; the basilican monastery of SS John and Paul (martyrs) by St Peter's; and the basilican monastery of St Stephen by St Lawrence without the wall. The sixth-century foundations were even more numerous: the nunneries 'near the place called the White Hens' (*ad Gallinas Albas*), near the church of St Agnes, and one near the baths of Agrippina. The men's houses, many of them basilican, included those of St Andrew cata Barbara, St Aristus, and those adjacent to the Lateran basilica; a basilican monastery near St Paul's was founded a little later. Of the sixth-century houses founded without relation to the saying of office in an existent basilica, there were three men's houses, three convents of nuns and a Greek monastery.[1]

---

[1] See Ferrari, *op. cit.,* for houses known to have been founded in the fifth century and onwards, together with maps of their siting; for that *ad clivum Scauri,* p. 138; for the *diaconiae,* p. 355; for basilican monasteries, under Vatican, Lateran, etc.

To none of these houses, however, did Pope Gregory, the spiritual father and patron of Augustine, feel himself called. He desired, with his great possessions, to found another monastery. He was, in 573, already in a great position, prefect of the city of Rome, to which post he had risen after long training in the civil service. As far as is known, he had lived hitherto in the family mansion or villa on the hill known as the Clivus Scauri: *clivus* was the word for mount, the Capitoline Mount being known as the Clivus Capitolinus. Gregory's paternal villa, with its *atrium* and *triclinium*, its cells, baths and garden, lay in the southern, less thickly populated part of the Roman city, between the Tiber and St John Lateran; it was near the road leading to Ostia, and its grounds adjoined the old library of Pope Agapitus, the *bibliotheca Agapiti*, probably no more than the ruins of an old building. There is an old reference to the cemetery of the monastery, perhaps outside the city walls, or possibly within the grounds of the villa in Rome; excavations in 1603 discovered eleven tombs, arranged in two levels in a kind of crypt beneath the oratory. There was a similar arrangement in the Greek monastery of St Saba, to the south of St Andrew's. Such crypts may represent an early practice evolved from catacomb burial: burial within the grounds of a villa was not yet allowed, and burial in such a catacomb-crypt would be lawful and yet keep the bodies of the monks within their own monastery.

The villa at any rate must have been of considerable size, to provide a dwelling for a body of monks from whom forty could be sent out on a single mission. Within the villa there were two oratories or chapels, dedicated to St Barbara and St Andrew. Gregory lived as monk in this monastery; Augustine had attained the position of *praepositus* in it by 596. No one knows whose influence led either man to 'conversion'; but monasticism was in the air, as the most completely dedicated life a Christian could live.

Gregory, then, entered his own monastery as novice; whether the written rules accessible to the abbot who trained him included the rule of St Benedict must be left an open question for lack of evidence. Benedict in his rule had commended his own arrangement of psalms for the office to any abbot who might choose to use them, and it was an arrangement assuming in some points knowledge of the forms of the Roman basilicas; the liturgical directions in the RSB were possibly useful to a Roman abbot. Moreover, the monastery *ad clivum Scauri* was well endowed and well founded. It is not impossible that a copy of the RSB should have reached it. But what Pope Gregory promised at profession was not obedience to the RSB, but renunciation of his goods and obedience to his abbot.

Augustine and the forty monks he took with him to England were all trained in Pope Gregory's monastery, where he himself had been a monk under Abbot Valentio from 574 to 578. Nothing is known to us of Augustine's family. Augustine was not a common baptismal name in Rome, and it is known that new and significant names were often taken on entry into the clerical or monastic orders; it is possible that the name Augustine was so taken. Names for abbots and bishops like Dominicus, Cumquodeus, Bonus ('the monk'), Concordius, Donatdeum, Evangelus (*diaconus*), Helias (Elias, priest abbot), Homobonus, Servus-Dei (*diaconus*), are not uncommon, and for abbesses and *ancillae dei*, Aluminosa, Bona, Domina, Dominica (*praeposita*). A letter of Gregory's mentions among others a bishop 'Redemptus' and an abbot 'Quod vult deus', names probably taken at a later stage than baptism. 'Augustine', if taken by a postulant on entry into the monastery, might argue the postulant's admiration for the great African doctor, or, more probably, the hope of the abbot who received him that here was a young man of some learning and ability, who might rise to a position in the monastery requiring learning and doctrine. Monks were received from all social classes, and even freed slaves (though the abbot must exercise great care to see that they had actually been freed); but boys and young men of education were given special training. St Benedict himself kept the oblate boys, Placid and Maurus, near himself for such special training, not leaving them to the care of the deans of Monte Cassino. Augustine may have had similar training.

He had, at any rate, been made *praepositus* by 596, a position he would hardly have attained till he had been a good number of years in the monastery and was known as a monk of judgment and virtue. The holder of such a position would have to be, not merely a good monk, but one trained in the holy scriptures and monastic rules, particularly the rule of his own monastery, and able to deal with the souls of his monks. Monks are not held together in an unnatural and austere life merely by an iron discipline, or the fear of hunger outside the monastery; they would, as a matter of fact, often be quite hungry inside the monastery. Their desire to 'run by a straight course to their Creator', to attain to that *apatheia* of the desert Fathers, had to be sustained by spiritual teaching. The term *praepositus* in the sixth century was sometimes used generally of any officer or ruler as set in his position by God, and sometimes specifically of the monk who was second in command in the monastery, as set in his position by the abbot. All monks were ranged in a monastery in order of their date of profession, and the older monastic rules sometimes assumed that, on the principle of seniority, the *secundus* in the monastery would be the abbot's principal assistant; if the abbot chose him for such an office not by seniority but for merit, he would be known as the *praepositus*.[1]

Augustine's work as *praepositus* of his monastery would have included helping his abbot to care for the landed endowment

[1] The word 'provost', *praepositus*, originally military, implied 'one set at the head of', e.g. a legion, a commission of legates, etc. by another and superior power. It was, in the sixth and earlier centuries, generally used of ecclesiastical, and even secular dignitaries, as officials appointed by God. Pope Gregory often used *praepositus* of himself and of the bishops, twice of a papal legate, and two or three times of the king or some high secular official; also, in this general sense of 'one set above', of an abbot, and also of a 'cloister provost'. The RM speaks of the monastery as headed by senior monks, each with a 'decade' of monks under him, though it does not call these officers 'deans' (*decani*), and it frequently calls them *praepositi*. St Benedict once speaks of the cloister dean as *praepositus*. It is clear that in the sixth century the word *praepositus* was often used generally, according to its literal meaning, and also applied particularly to the second in command of a monastery.

In the appointment of an assistant, it appears from Gregory's letters that the abbot might follow the principle of seniority, if the senior monk were fit to have the custody and ordering of the brethren, and were skilful in gaining souls. But if there were no senior monk who would well fill this place, and there were a monk, even low in seniority, and he were of good monastic life and vigorous in the fear of God, then he should be designated *praepositus*, not for his seniority but his usefulness and suitable behaviour; 'Let him,' said Gregory, 'by his own example spread among the brethren the norm of good observance.' This was, in fact, in accordance with ancient monastic tradition, and St Benedict's recommendation that an abbot himself should be elected 'not by seniority, but according to the merit of his life'. That Augustine, and not the abbot of the house, should have been chosen for the English mission, is easily explicable. Not only was the abbot probably too old to undertake successfully the long journey to England, and the planting of the English church through years of great difficulty; but his monks at St Andrews had sworn obedience to him personally, and Gregory seems to have been loath, even when an abbot had proved himself foolish and incapable, to break such a link.

of the abbey, on which the feeding of the brethren depended. He must keep a watch over the lay *conductores* or stewards of the villas of the endowment, for his monastery had lands near the twenty-fifth milestone on the Via Tiburtina, in the Campus Maior, and outside the Porta Maggiore. The monks (and their guests) lived on the food provided from these lands. Augustine would not be expected to conduct any necessary litigation about monastic lands in the Roman law courts himself, for Pope Gregory mentions in one of his letters that such conduct was unsuitable for monks: they must get a notary to represent them in the courts. But abbots and *praepositi* must have a certain knowledge of Roman law, such as would enable them to safeguard the monasteries' possessions; they would have this knowledge if they had attended the rhetor's school and learned 'rhetoric', the subject in the liberal arts which afforded some instruction in Roman law.

Augustine, as *praepositus*, must have had enough knowledge to understand, keep in safe custody, and deal with the document by which Gregory added to the endowment of his monastery certain lands which had come to him by way of a legacy. Augustine must actually have seen this document, which was in the form of a private charter. Gregory issued it on 28 December, 587, when he had returned from Constantinople and was again working as papal deacon. It was drafted by a notary, and illustrates both the manner in which life in Gregory's monastery was sustained, and the level of ability and knowledge needed by the abbot and *praepositus*. It was addressed to 'the holy and venerable monastery of Saint Andrew the apostle built on my own land which is called the Clivus Scauri, in which Maximianus is the most reverend abbot, and through him to the same venerable monastery. I, Gregory, unworthy deacon of the apostolic see, send greeting. . . . I Gregory, "servus servorum dei", grant, yield, hand over and deliver from my lawful possession (*iure*) to your lawful possession, and I transfer to your dominion, four whole measures [of land] of the three farms known as the Laverian, Speian and Ancessan with their villages and appurtenances, even if they are called by another name, with their slaves and *coloni* and all rights over them and ownership of them, with houses and walled appendages adjoining or adjacent, with woods, fields, meadows, pastures, sally gardens and plantations, vines, olives, trees that bear apples or other fruit or that do not bear fruit, wells, springs, streams of water and all their permanent boundaries and all things belonging to these four measures of land, inscribed above as the Laverian, Speian and Ancessan with the villages . . . which lie more or less at the twenty-fifth milestone from Rome on the Via Tiburtina, in the Tiburtine territory. . . .' The remainder of the long document specifies the lands and their holders among which the lands donated lie, and guarantees that Gregory's heirs and successors shall never claim the land under cover of guile or fiction: he promises that his heirs and successors shall maintain the grant of this written charter, which Gregory has bidden the notary Deusdedit to write, which he has signed with his own hand, and for which he has obtained the signature of witnesses. The attestations and signatures of three witnesses follow, all of them stating that Gregory has signed in their presence and they in his; the four include a *vir clarissimus*, a notary socially graded as a *vir honestus*, and a *lector* holding his title from the church of St Mary; we are here in the presence of a Roman noble, a notary of the *scrinium* and a young clerk of the papal household.

Augustine as *praepositus* must have been not only able to deal with and keep in safe custody private charters such as this, but he must have been indeed the helper and 'solace' of his abbot in matters spiritual and secular. As the monk most likely to become abbot himself later he must have been not only able to deal with souls but also prudent in dealing with outsiders and in the reception of guests. He must have been able to make decisions in the course of any mission entrusted to him by the abbot outside the monastery. Yet he was as much bound by obedience to his abbot as any other monk. The promise of the conversion of manners and obedience had been made into the hands of his abbot and it was a relationship that no promotion within the monastery could modify.

The position and power of the *praepositus* together with the fact that Benedict preferred to govern his monastery through deans, while Gregory assumed that a *praepositus* was more useful to an abbot, has provoked comment. Gregory, indeed, in one case urged the appointment of a *praepositus*, and himself sent Augustine to England as *praepositus*, though he soon appointed him as abbot to strengthen his power over his hesitating monks. There is, however, no real difficulty here, for the word *praepositus* had in the sixth century an elastic signification.

The title, which Augustine already held, was in effect the obvious one for him to hold as leader of the band of monks sent by Gregory on the mission to England. It was bound to be temporary; the missionary monks were still bound to monastic obedience, for none of them had as yet been taken out of the monastic order to become clerks; Lawrence, the one priest among them, was still a monk; and monks owed obedience to someone. It would seem to have been the pope's intention to await the foundation of a monastery in England before the appointment of an abbot, but, in fact, circumstances forced his hand.

Augustine's work, before and after he left Italy, must have included not only spiritual direction and legal responsibilities, but the day to day direction of the liturgy. He was responsible for the community mass and the *opus dei*. He must have been already a priest, for there is no record of his receiving the priesthood before his consecration as bishop later. The saying of the divine office involved settling the timetable of the community, the order in which the psalms were to be recited and the lessons read. The short lessons of the day hours may well have been traditional in Rome, following the observance of the Lateran choir; but the long lessons of the night office would depend on the will of abbot or *praepositus*. No doubt one of the reasons why the Benedictine rule was found so useful by those acquainted with it was the detailed prescriptions Benedict gave for the psalms to be sung at each office, the lessons read and the canticles sung (RSB, chapters VIII to XVIII).

As to the term *opus dei* and its contemporary meaning: in Augustine's day the phrase was already used in the restricted sense of the divine office, but older and more general meanings were common. Pope Gregory still used it frequently with a general meaning: in the old scriptural sense, 'This is the work of God, that ye believe on him whom he hath sent.' Those who spread the Christian faith were, in a scriptural sense, engaged on the *opus dei*: the phrase covered both their apostolate and their liturgy. Gregory, however, used the term *opus dei* in more than one sense: 'the *opus dei* . . . is to collect and recall to the joys of the light eternal the souls whom he has created', that is: the apostolate is an *opus dei*; at other times he uses it of the whole creation of God, and of the whole life of faith in Christ: for St Paul had exhorted Christians to be 'ever abounding in the work of God' (*abundantes in opere dei semper*). In early times, and up to the sixth century, the *opus dei* had come to mean particularly the ideal and ascetic life in Christ, the whole monastic life, with its fasting, offering of hospitality to strangers, and 'continual prayer', and it was even used especially of the coenobitic life. The phrase could still be used in all these senses in Augustine's day.

But *opus dei* had also acquired the specialised meaning of the monastic office before the days of Benedict and Gregory, and of this special meaning Gregory could scarcely have been ignorant.[1]

He certainly used the phrase *opus dei* occasionally in the liturgical sense, either from familiarity with the RSB or with other sources. The association in his mind of the missionary and liturgical meanings of *opus dei* is of some interest, in that he did send monks on this apostolic mission.

The letters of Pope Gregory are a mine of information about church life in his day and the world in which Augustine lived at Rome. Gregory often wrote to, or referred to, a *praepositus* as the *secundus* in a monastery, and of *praepositi* who were spiritual rulers of some sort, bishops or monastic deans. His letters illuminate various aspects of the *vita monachica* as Augustine knew it; he wrote about admission to the life, seclusion within the monastery, passage from the monastic to the clerical servitude, the keeping of archives, the written *privilegia* granted to monasteries, the infringement of monastic rights by seculars

---

[1] Caesarius of Arles (d. 542) used it in this sense, as did the Magister in the RM, the rule of Bishop Aurelian, written between 546 and 548, and St Benedict himself. Moreover, the Roman deacon Pelagius (d. 561) translated the five books of the *Vitae Patrum* from Greek into Latin, and translated σύναξις by *opus dei*. In the fifth book he has a story where an Egyptian anchorite's prayers are called *opus dei*; certain monks and pilgrims are related to have visited the Egyptian fathers; he says:

And another old man came to a certain father, who was cooking a small portion of vegetables. And he said to the old man: Let us perform the *opus dei*, and then let us eat. And one of them recited the whole psalter, and the other recited by heart in due order two of the greater prophets. And when the day had dawned, the old man who had come departed, and they forgot to partake of food.

and sometimes by bishops, the rule and defence of nuns, the care for dispersed monks whose monastery had been sacked and who were now living irregularly and even dissolutely and who ought to be gathered together again into a monastery by their bishop. The letters open a window on the world in which Augustine lived and whose standards and traditions he was to attempt to transplant, as accompaniments of the Christian faith, to the cold, pagan and no doubt barbarous world of the Anglo-Saxons.

Among these letters we find, for instance, Gregory writing in 591 to the rector of the papal lands in the Campania, saying that he must make monks who wander from monastery to monastery return to their own houses, and make them also give up the property, personal or otherwise, which they have once renounced; the souls of monks that perish shall be required at the hands of their rulers. If a man comes to monastic life from the clerical order, it shall not be lawful for him to return to his former church or to any other church; unless he be so good a monk that the bishop now deem him fit for the priesthood.

In 592 he wrote to an abbot John, who had asked leave to ordain Brother Boniface *praepositus* in his monastery, that he should so ordain him: 'And I very much wonder why this has not been done before, for I sent him to you for this purpose.'

To the abbot of Rimini he wrote that the secundus had complained to him that, as the abbot had no *praepositus*, he had the sole burden of ruling the brethren. If the *secundus* had been found skilful in arranging and ordering the cells (small groups of brethren) and in gaining souls, he should at once be made *praepositus*. But if not, and if by God's will there should be a monk, even in the lowest grade by seniority but of good life and full of monastic vigour, he should be promoted, his new position being due to his usefulness and fitness for the work.

To another abbot he wrote that monks who set themselves in opposition to their *praepositi* showed themselves to be no true monks: 'They scorn to be the slaves of God.'

In 598 Gregory arranged some complicated legal business for his own house *ad clivum Scauri*. He wrote to Abbot Candidus saying that, as he wished to avoid further litigation for the monastery, he had personally confirmed the arrangement between Candidus and the *magister militum*, Maurentius, a high secular official. Maurentius's brother John had been a monk in the house and died there: Maurentius, apparently, had made some difficulty about handing over to the monastery the estates his brother, as a monk, had renounced. But he had now made a corporal oath (sworn, touching a holy relic) that he had now defrauded the monastery of nothing, but handed over all his brother's estate; Gregory has had a written 'precept' or document made, recording this, for the monastery.

Gregory's letter to Maurus, abbot of the monastery of St Pancras, near the Lateran basilica, is of interest, perhaps specially with relation to Durovernum, because Augustine or his successor chose to dedicate to St Pancras the church built within the grounds of the monastery of SS Peter and Paul. This may have arisen simply because Pope Gregory had sent Augustine *pallia* or *vela* laid against the tomb of St Pancras in this church at Rome, or because the Roman monks at Durovernum were familiar with the basilican monastery on the Lateran. The origins of the house cannot be precisely established, but it was the earliest of Lateran monasteries, and Gregory in the *Dialogues*,[1] written in 593 and 594, says that Valentinian, the disciple of Benedict, had ruled it for many years: apparently, he was now dead. For a time, apparently, the church reverted to the care of priests, for in 594 Gregory wrote to the monk Maurus, establishing him as abbot of St Pancras. He said that the priests to whose care the church had been committed had neglected it, 'so that the people, coming on the Lord's day to celebrate the solemnities of the mass and finding no priest there have retired murmuring'. Gregory has decided to remove the priests and appoint a congregation of monks for this church, with the abbot to have care and charge of the church. He has decided to set Maurus there as abbot, and, lest the divine mysteries be lacking, Maurus shall provide a priest for the pilgrims, to celebrate solemn mass. 'And this above all things shall be your charge, that there, before the most holy body of St Pancras the *opus dei* shall daily without any uncertainty be performed.'

Gregory's letters are full of directions for abbots and bishops

[1] See for the Dialogues, Moricca, Dialogi, lib. ii, and for a translation, O. P. Zimmerman and B. R. Avery, *Life and Miracles of St Benedict*, Collegeville, Minnesota, 1949

and, long before Bede's famous letter to Archbishop Egbert of York about false or 'feigned' minsters, Gregory had written about such an abuse in Italy. He wrote to John, bishop of Ravenna, that he has heard that in certain places in John's episcopal see there are places consecrated as monasteries 'which have now been made the dwellings of secular clergy or even laymen, who feign themselves to be living as religious and who claim to be rulers of monasteries. Through such monastic life is destroyed.' Let John correct this.

Augustine, when he arrived in Britain, knew nothing of Anglo-Saxon society, except as it resembled that of the Franks, through whom he had made his long journey; but he knew a good deal about bishops, clergy and monks.

CHAPTER 2

# The Sending of the Mission to England

POPE GREGORY'S knowledge of the Anglo-Saxons to whom he
sent Augustine must have been limited: but he knew, at any
rate, that they were pagans. The story that Bede tells of his
having seen Anglo-Saxon boys, war-captives, exposed for sale
by slave dealers in the market-place, seems to have come to
Bede from Anglian sources: it is a story that might have been
handed down in the *familia* at Canterbury, and told him by the
Canterbury priest Nothelm, on one of his visits to Jarrow.
There is nothing improbable in Gregory's pun on the words
*Angli* and *angeli,* or the name of the Anglian boys' king, Ælle,
and the 'Hallel' which, Gregory said, they ought to sing in
heaven.

That Gregory's interest in the English was aroused by the
slave boys is supported by a letter of September 595, in his
Register; the notaries of his *scrinium* kept copies of his letters.
The pope wrote to Candidus the priest, whom he was sending
to rule the patrimony (landed estates) of the Roman church in
Gaul, and bade him spend the revenue he would receive in
Gaul itself; for not only were Gallic shillings (which were
smaller) unexpendable in Italy, but the see of Peter would be
held in greater respect if such revenue were spent, not for the
profit of the rector himself or the Roman church, but for the
good of the people of the patrimony. Candidus was to buy
clothes for the poor and Anglian boys of seventeen or eighteen
years of age, that they might be 'given to God in monasteries';
that is, that these slave boys or young men, brought by traders
to the great slave-market at Marseilles, and now 'offered to
God' might become monks. Money obtained from any other
source by Candidus, Gregory said, should be similarly used for
clothes for the poor and to buy slave boys. 'And because they
are pagans who come from that country,' he continued, 'send
a priest with them, lest they fall sick on the journey, and if they

23

look to him as if they were going to die, he should baptise them.'

The young slaves bought by Candidus had no long training in Rome, for ten months only after Gregory wrote this letter we find that Augustine's monks had already travelled to the old Roman 'provincia' at the mouth of the Rhône, stayed some time at the monastery of Lérins, a short time with the bishop of Aix-en-Provence, and sent Augustine back to remonstrate with the pope and receive the command to proceed with the mission. Gregory sent also a bunch of commendatory letters, all dated July 596 and some of them 22 July 596.

The commendatory letters were all carried by Augustine on his return to Provence: none had been sent originally. The *scrinium* at Rome had knowledge of the old cities of Roman Gaul, but very little knowledge of the half-barbarian Frankish kings who struggled for power with raids and assassinations. When Augustine returned from Lérins, Gregory learned of personages to whom letters might usefully be addressed, but even so, only personages of southern and central Gaul: there are no commendatory letters to bishops or princes farther north than Autun and Tours.

Gregory had little precise knowledge of the struggles of the Merovingian kings in Gaul, or even of the names of the bishops in the central and northern sees; lists of the sees themselves were of course kept in his *scrinium*. He might take it that any king whose name he knew would receive a papal letter with respect; but he suspected that in the kings' bloody and fratricidal struggles, help given to Augustine by one side would mean hostility from the other. He had heard however of Queen Brunhild as a good catholic princess, and powerful.

We, however, know more of the fratricidal struggles of the Frankish kings than did Gregory. Clovis the Frank had been baptised in 506 and ruled all Gaul, with Paris as his capital. When his fourth son, Lothar I, died in 561, the old Roman unity of 'the Gauls' was lost; Lothar's four sons divided up his territories. One son, Charibert, ruled Paris; his daughter, Bertha, was sent over to marry the young Kentish prince, Æthelberht, in 560; the link between Paris and Canterbury was maintained by the cross-Channel trade. When Charibert died in 567, his brothers divided his lands, even dividing in thirds his capital city of Paris. One brother, Sigebert, then ruled the north-eastern Frankish territories from Metz, and he made a splendid marriage with the Visigothic princess, Brunhild, a well-educated lady, very beautiful, statesmanlike, Christian and ruthless; she was admired not only in her husband's kingdom of 'Austrasia' but in all the Frankish courts. Another brother, Chilperic, ruled 'Neustria' from Soissons; he fancied himself as a Latinist and insisted that four extra letters should be added to the alphabet to express the sounds of the Latin language adequately; he wrote Latin verse that Gregory of Tours maintained had false quantities. He was fierce and cruel, and Gregory of Tours called him the 'Nero and Herod' of his day, implying that he equalled the stock examples of ruthless cruelty in both pagan and Christian history. His violence started the bitter feud which brought a civil war, marked by murder and assassination, which divided Neustria and Austrasia for forty years, in the course of which Augustine made his two journeys through Gaul.

Some knowledge of the quarrel and its cause must probably have reached Bertha in Kent, for Queen Brunhild was her aunt, and merchants passed between Canterbury and Metz. In some form she probably heard the story of how King Chilperic, who had a wife of his own (and a low-born mistress, Fredegond, to whom he was attached), put his wife away and married a Visigothic princess, Galswintha, the sister of Bertha's aunt, Brunhild. Galswintha was a very fine lady, in the Byzantine manner, and she objected to her husband's continued devotion to Fredegond: as a result, Galswintha was found in short order strangled on her bed. Brunhild never forgave the crime, which according to the old pagan blood feud she was bound to avenge; the blood feud between the royal houses of Neustria and Austrasia was bitter. In central and southern Gaul, King Guntram ruled Orleans and Burgundy more peacefully.

Assassination accompanied tyranny in the north: in 575 Sigebert was murdered by two slaves of Fredegond, and Queen Brunhild had hard work to hold Austrasia for her son, Childebert II; Guntram supported her. In 584 Chilperic himself was stabbed in the forest of Chelles, near Paris, and Queen Fredegond ruled Neustria in the name of her infant son, Lothar II. In 593 King Guntram died, and was succeeded by Brunhild's son, Childebert II, whom he had adopted as his

3

heir, and when this Childebert died (life was short for Merovingian princes in those days), Brunhild took upon herself, in
addition to the defence of Austrasia, that of the kingdom of
Burgundy: Childebert's two sons, Theodebert (Thibert) now
ruled Austrasia, and Theodoric (Thierry), Burgundy. But real
power lay in the hands of Brunhild. She outlived Fredegond,
who died in 597, and was herself defeated only in 613; she was
killed by the cruel old 'horsedeath' which the Huns had brought
to Europe and taught the Franks. When Augustine, then, was
travelling up through the Frankish kingdoms it was through a
Burgundy under the protection of Brunhild, and a Paris where
Queen Fredegond had only a year to live; the pope had sent
her no commendatory letter, but there were old links between
Paris and Canterbury and presumably Augustine and his
monks followed the way taken by the merchants without
difficulty.

Bede, who knew little of Augustine's journey, tells us simply
that Pope Gregory, 'a man outstanding both in doctrine and
action', sent Augustine the servant of God (*servus dei*: monk)
and many other God-fearing monks with him to preach the
word of God to the English, 'about a hundred and fifty years
from the coming of the English into Britain'. Augustine and his
party began their journey in 596 in obedience to the papal
command, and, as we know from Gregory's letters, stayed
with the bishop of Aix-en-Provence and presumably for longer
in the island monastery of Lérins. At some point in their
journey, Bede relates, the monks became alarmed: 'They sent
back Augustine, whom Gregory had thought fit to be ordained
bishop for them if they should be well received by the king.'
Augustine recounted to Gregory the kindness he had received
from the bishop of Aix and the charity and virtue of the monks
of Lérins, in some detail, and (presumably) the names of those
likely to afford the papal missionaries some protection, if letters
could be given him to present to them. He would also have
heard something of the regions the party must pass through
from other travellers, and the pilgrims who frequented the
monastery of Lérins, which lay in its small archipelago to the
south of the Alpes Maritimes (near the modern Grasse).

Bede here quotes Pope Gregory's letter of encouragement
to the disheartened monks, telling them he has made Augustine

their abbot: a letter which would be carefully preserved at Canterbury, and a copy of it was sent by Nothelm to Bede. The letter runs:

> Since it is better not to begin good works than to have second thoughts and withdraw from those that are begun, you must, my dearest sons, zealously complete the good work you have begun. Neither the toil of the journey, nor the tongues of evil speakers should deter you; therefore carry out with all instancy and fervour what you have begun by God's help, knowing that the greater the labour, the greater the reward of eternal glory. Humbly obey therefore in all things Augustine the *praepositus,* whom moreover we have appointed to be your abbot, knowing that whatever at his command ye fulfil will be for the good of your own souls. May almighty God protect you by his grace and grant me to behold in the eternal country the fruit of your labour, for although I cannot labour with you, I do indeed desire to do so: may I share in the joy of your reward.

Augustine brought with him also a sheaf of commendatory letters. They asked for protection and aid on the journey for the band of monks, on the grounds that they would be engaged on the evangelical work of converting the pagans. They explained Gregory's intervention in a matter which should be the concern of the bishops of the Franks, as the neighbours of the Anglo-Saxons. Moreover, in Roman days Britain had belonged to the praetorian prefecture of the Gauls, whose capital city was Arles: the metropolitan of Arles had once had a shadowy supervision of the British churches. In 596 the bishop of Arles was metropolitan of the old 'provincia'; in the kingdom of Burgundy to the north two great cities rivalled Arles, Lyons and Autun, with Lyons claiming the old position of metropolitan, and Autun, whose bishop, Syagrius, was a strong supporter of Brunhild and King Thibert, trying to claim equal honour. All these bishops might resent Gregory's concern with the Anglo-Saxons, regarded as inhabiting their outlying pagan territories, although in fact the only Gallic bishop who had concerned himself with the lands beyond the Channel had been Germanus of Auxerre. A bishop of this city, far to the north of the Rhône, and on the line of the cross-Channel trade, from Paris to Kent and the Solent, would be better acquainted with conditions across the Channel than his brothers in the south. Gregory now explained his missionary efforts on the ground of the neglect of the Frankish bishops to undertake such work.

Gregory wrote also three letters to secular rulers. To Queen Brunhild he wrote 'that he well knows of her zeal for the Christian religion, and in confidence of this he may say that news has come to him that the people of the English through God's grace desire to be Christian, but the bishops in their neighbourhood have no pastoral zeal towards them. Lest therefore their souls perish forever, do you, as far as possible, help Augustine the monk, bearer of this letter, whose zeal and care are well known to us, that through him we may know of the intentions of the English and of their conversion, through your efforts.'

To the kings Thierry and Thibert, Brunhild's grandsons, he wrote a joint letter: Since he knew them to be conspicuous and whole-hearted Christians, desiring to convert their own subjects to the faith, he has presumed their interest in the Anglo-Saxons, of whom news has reached him that they piteously desire to be converted to the Christian faith, but the neighbouring bishops neglect them and the desires of the English fail to kindle them. Therefore he has taken thought to send the monk Augustine, bearer of this letter, and other monks, and he has enjoined them to take priests from the neighbourhood with him.

To one more secular power Gregory directed his appeal: he saluted Arigius, patrician of Gaul, and ruler, in effect, of the province of Massilia, and asked his help on the journey for Augustine the monk and the monks with him.

Where Augustine delivered these letters remains uncertain: the seat of Brunhild's power was Metz, quite out of the way of Augustine's travels, but he may have had occasion to approach her in Burgundy, in Lyons or Autun; King Thierry also he would expect to find in Burgundy, Arigius in the province.

The commendatory letters Gregory sent to bishops, and those which he bore with him, were equally vital to Augustine.

Gregory wrote to Protasius, bishop of Aix-en-Province, of whose devotion to the apostolic see he well knew; he had heard from Augustine the bearer of the letter, of his zeal and good works.

To Stephen, abbot of Lérins, he wrote with gratitude of all
the kindness the abbot has shown to Augustine and his monks
earlier; Augustine, the bearer of this letter, has told him of his
lively affection, and of how in his congregation the priests and
deacons and indeed the whole congregation live together in
peace and unity. Let him continue to guard those committed to
him against the wiles of the enemy. He thanks him for the gift
of spoons and rings which he has sent him for the use of the
poor.

To Vergilius, bishop of Arles and metropolitan of 'the Gauls',
he wrote commending Augustine the monk, bearer of the
letter, and the monks with him.

When the monks had made their way northwards along the
road to the east of the Rhône to Vienne and Lyons, and from
along the west bank to Chalon and Autun, they might present as
credentials the letter Gregory addressed jointly to Desiderius of
Vienne and Syagrius of Autun. On another occasion, Gregory
reprehended Desiderius for too great enthusiasm in teaching
classical literature: could the same mouth at the same time sing
the praises of Jove and Christ? And with Syagrius he also had
other dealings, suspecting him at one time of being implicated
with heretics, but later commending him for the help he
actually, on this first journey, gave Augustine. The pope wrote
to Brunhild, in September 597, saying that: 'We have heard by
the relation of many of the faithful how indeed your excellency
yourself has treated Augustine our brother and co-bishop.'
Queen Brunhild's and Bishop Syagrius's kindness indeed helped
Augustine on his original journey to Kent (and on his journey
back to Arles to be consecrated bishop: by September 597 he
had been so consecrated).

Thus there is evidence in Gregory's letters for Augustine's
journey as far as Autun; from there onwards there is only the
likelihood that he followed the old Roman roads northwards to
Sens, Paris, Rouen or Amiens, and Quentavic. The letters sent
to him in 601, when Augustine had established himself in
Canterbury and asked for more helpers, include commendatory
letters to the bishops of Chalon-sur-Saône, Paris, Angers and
Rouen; they suggest that Augustine had visited these cities
already. Though the hostility between Brunhild, Augustine's
patron, and Queen Fredegond at Paris was so bitter, it is likely

that a band of monks, headed by Augustine, could pass through Paris, lodging in the monasteries and xenodochia, without attracting much notice.

Eventually Augustine and his monks and interpreters crossed the Channel, presumably in more than one boat, and sailed northwards, past the old Roman port of Dover and the South Foreland, and into the mouth of the river Stour, which separates the 'island of Thanet' from the Kentish mainland, and which Bede calls the Wantsum. Higher up the Stour the Watling Street from Dover crossed the river at a ford, the ford which was the geographical reason for the siting of the Roman Durovernum, and where other Roman roads converged. At this city, Durovernum Cantiacorum, the *bretwalda* Æthelberht had his residence; it had indeed been the site of the settlements of Jutish mercenaries even before the invaders had conquered the Roman provincials of the region.

Augustine, however, could not sail on unannounced up river to the capital; instead, he sent a messenger to say 'that they had come from Rome and bore good tidings, indeed, the best of tidings, which should bring to those who welcomed them eternal joy in the heavens, and an endless future kingdom with the living God'. And the king bade them remain on the island of Thanet where they had landed; 'and he bade all things necessary to be supplied to them till he should see what he should do about them'. For some knowledge of the Christian faith had reached him many years before, 'when he had received the Christian woman Bertha, of the royal race of the Franks, to be his wife. For he had received her from her parents on condition that she should be allowed to keep inviolate the rite of her faith and religion, together with the bishop Liuthard whom they had given her as the supporter of her faith'. Liudhard had been a bishop, customarily at least fifty years old, in 560; he must have been an old man in 597, or, more probably, he had died.

'Some days later,' Bede continues,[1] 'Æthelberht came to the island, and taking his seat in the open air, commanded Augustine and his companions to come to confer with him there. For he was cautious, according to the old custom of augury,

---

[1] For his famous description of the interview, see Plummer's ed. of the *Historia Ecclesiastica*, I, p. 43

lest they should gain an entry into a house, and if they were possessed of any evil art, deceive him by its power. But they, using not the strength of demons but the divine protection, came bearing a silver cross, and the picture of the Saviour painted on a board, singing litanies for their own eternal salvation and that of those to whom they came. And when at his command they were seated, they preached the word of life to him and all those in his company; and the king answered and said:

'These indeed are fair words and promises that ye bring; but because they are new and to us uncertain, I cannot give my assent to them and abandon those to which for so long a time I with all the people of the English have been faithful. But since you have come here as travellers from afar and desire to communicate to us also those things which you believe true and for our good, we have no wish to harm you in any way, but rather to receive you with kindly hospitality; we shall be careful to provide you with the food necessary to you; nor do we forbid you to associate with you all whom ye can by the preaching of your faith and religion.

'And he gave them a dwelling house [*mansionem*] in the city of Durovernum, which was the metropolis of his whole kingdom; nor did he fall short of his promise to supply their corporal needs or give them licence to preach. For it is said [Bede is here relying on what had been told him by Nothelm the priest about the early history of the mission], that when they were approaching the city of Durovernum, according to their custom with the holy cross and the painted picture of the great king, our Lord Jesus Christ, they sang loudly and clearly these words: "We pray thee, O Lord, in thy mercy, take away thine anger from us and thy wrath from this city, and from thy holy house: for we have sinned. Alleluia." '

Augustine had reached the first stage of his mission: he had been received by Æthelberht. What sort of a man then was this king, and what sort of a city was this half-ruined Durovernum, where Augustine had been given a residence? He knew Rome, where palaces, houses and basilicas were still built of blocks of marble and squared stone; Rome, with its old temples fallen into decay, its marble statues, its catacombs where St Jerome had walked, 'free among the dead', and been amazed at the

weight of history pressing in on him; where there were still
manuscripts and libraries and learned men; where Roman
lawyers safeguarded private life and goods with written instruments, and the prefect of the city was still a Roman magistrate.
He had travelled up through Gaul where the Frankish barbarians, Christians since Clovis, lived on in houses that still
lined the streets of the Roman town, where the town plan was
the rectangular gridwork laid out by the army surveyor in the
years following Caesar and his conquests; where bishops and
counts had notaries who wrote their letters and transacted their
business. How much of all this, how much of what was
civilisation to Augustine, was left among the people of the
English?

Æthelberht he had seen as the warrior overlord, the *bretwalda*
of all the Angles and Saxons up to the Humber. He had, after
his arrival in Canterbury, heard the *scopa*, the bard, sing his
praises on his little hand harp at the feast to which he had been,
at length, invited. Though Augustine could not understand the
singing, the Frankish interpreter, who could at any rate make a
guess at it, said (one may suppose) that the singer praised the
king as the heir of the royal line of the Oiscingas; he sang the
praises of Hengist, who first brought his people to Kent; of
Horsa his brother, who fell in battle with the Britons, and was
buried where a fine stone monument, with his name carved upon
it, marks the spot; he sang of Oisc, Hengist's son, of Octa, his
grandson, Eormanric, his great-grandson, the father of
Æthelberht himself. All this line of kings sprang from the gods,
yes, from Woden himself, the All-Father, whose priests had
many sanctuaries and were bitterly opposed to Augustine's
coming and his influence on the king. Augustine would have a
lot of trouble with these priests.

Æthelberht himself Augustine had seen as a middle-aged
warrior, his tunic clasped on each shoulder by a fine brooch of
cloisonné work, his belt fastened with a buckle of gold and fine
enamel, his sword with its chased handle hanging from the
belt but, as he sat in peaceful conference, its end protected by a
short metal sheath. One of the king's companions, a young
'eorl' held the king's shield, with its very fine metal ornaments
on the face, and on the inner side a leather strap and handle to
enable the holder to grip it.

Æthelberht indeed, the interpreter said, had been a good fighter: he had defeated the West Saxons and their king, Ceawlin, who up till his defeat had been reckoned *bretwalda* of the English; King Rædwald of the East Angles seemed to be a good fighter, but he was very young and no danger as yet to Æthelberht; in fact, the interpreter continued, Æthelberht was the strongest king of these barbarous English, and no doubt one of the reasons for this was his patronage by King Charibert of Paris, who had let him marry his daughter years ago. She is a pious lady, the interpreter rambled on, as you know from the welcome which I interpreted to you; she cannot understand your speech however, though it delights her to hear your fine Roman Latin, when you celebrate the holy mysteries. She has a very fine brooch, Father, and a chatelaine with a comb, and keys hanging from it; I doubt if you could buy as fine a brooch in Paris. The ladies of Paris might consider the design outlandish, yet I think they would be envious.

Augustine had been offered Frankish wine at the banquet, poured through a strainer, for it had been much shaken in its journey across the Channel. Wine was for royal banquets only, for it was dear; Æthelberht supplied Augustine and his monks with beer brewed from the royal barley strips in the fields, for beer he considered one of the necessities of life. Beer, however, Augustine liked little, accustomed as he was to drink sparingly of the red wine of the Campagna; but he and his monks drank it, for monks are trained not to have likes and dislikes about food. For the rest, English bread and English cheese were good enough, and well suited to monks; of these, the king had certain supplies sent to him from the royal lands in Kent. It would be well, Augustine thought, since they were now settled in Kent, if a written deed could be made out, securing these lands, and he told this to the interpreter, who agreed with him. 'But,' he said, 'these people do not use written deeds; the king will proclaim that he has given you certain lands in his council, which these people call the folk moot, and the men of his council will bear witness that the land has been given. If, indeed, Father,' he said, 'the king makes such a gift to you and to the monks for ever: for this is unusual, and moreover, Father, you have not yet converted the king. It is true that he loves his queen, and he thinks your new religion very civilised and progressive; he thinks your gods are perhaps more powerful than his; but many of his people would consider such a change very unlucky. The king's sister Ricula, they said, married the father of Saeberht, king of the East Saxons, who come at the king's war call, and they have a very great temple on the hill of Harrow; the East Saxons are very suspicious of you, Father, because, if you baptised Æthelberht, Saeberht would have to enter the waters of baptism too; and then, what would become of the priest of Harrow and all the servants of the temple? Of course, the Kentish men have sanctuaries of their own, up on the hills; but Harrow is a very great sanctuary. I have heard strange rumours of the sacrifice they offer on the altar there at dawn when the sun rises at the summer solstice.' 'The king tells me,' said Augustine, 'that this is not so. Do not spread this rumour among the monks.' 'No, no, Father,' said the interpreter, 'that would be foolish, and anyway they will have heard it from somebody. Monks always hear things. As you say, Father, we must pray. The monks pray so much, God will surely hear them.'

The town of Durovernum, where Augustine had been brought after his meeting with the king by the Wantsum, and where he was to establish his see, had been inhabited by the Belgic invaders who came before Caesar's raid on Britain in 54 B.C., or, at least, the hill-top stronghold of Bigbury Wood above it had been inhabited. It may have been the Belgic fortress stormed by Caesar in 54 B.C. Caesar says nothing of Canterbury itself, but large quantities of pottery of the years 10–40 suggest that there was a Belgic hut-site at Canterbury before his coming. After the Romans had established peace and order in Kent, Canterbury was formally laid out by the surveyors, and became the capital of the eastern part of Belgic Kent.

Even after the Saxon invasions the name Durovernum survived: an 'abbot of Durovernum' is mentioned as having attended the council of Paris in 614. Under Roman rule, the local magistrates, the decurions, erected the public buildings surrounding the city's centre, the Forum, the large market square with its basilica. This large colonnaded hall for public business, built on a stepped plinth so that speakers could address the townsmen outside as from a raised platform, ran along one side of the Forum; the other three sides of the square

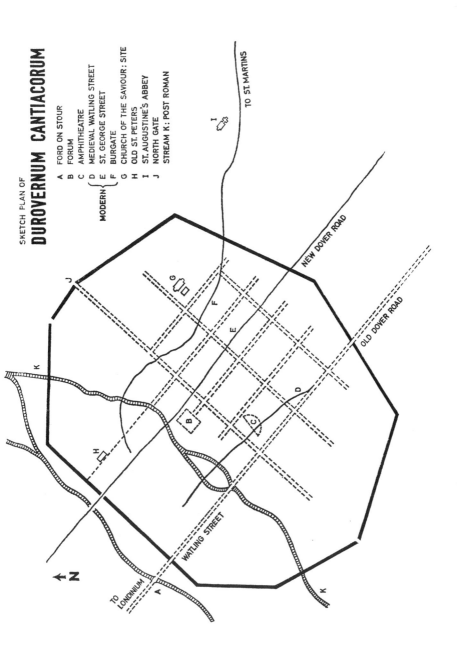

SKETCH PLAN OF
# DUROVERNUM CANTIACORUM

A  FORD ON STOUR
B  FORUM
C  AMPHITHEATRE
MODERN { D  MEDIEVAL WATLING STREET
         E  ST. GEORGE STREET
F  BURGATE
G  CHURCH OF THE SAVIOUR: SITE
H  OLD ST. PETERS
I  ST. AUGUSTINE'S ABBEY
J  NORTH GATE
STREAM K: POST ROMAN

TO ST. MARTINS

NEW DOVER ROAD

OLD DOVER ROAD

WATLING STREET

TO LONDINIUM

N

would have been covered by colonnades of shops and bath buildings. The Roman wall, or its ruins, would have been visible to Augustine, for it survived as the circuit of medieval and modern Canterbury. Some indication of the grid-iron plan of the Roman city must have survived in a half-ruined condition in Augustine's time, though the Cantware had settled in the city's ruins without preserving the street plan. The Watling Street still ran through the city, and passed close to the early Roman amphitheatre. This had been built adjacent to the early, unwalled, Roman city, and then enclosed within its walls after some rising had made such a defence advisable.

The remains of at least three Christian churches built in Roman times would seem to have survived till Augustine's day: Bede states that Æthelberht, after his baptism, gave the bishop leave both to build and restore churches. There is evidence that he was able to restore three such churches, as well as planning to build certain new ones.

The first church lay adjacent to the *mansio* which Æthelberht had granted him; Bede says that Augustine 'restored, with the royal aid, in the place where he had been given an episcopal see, the church which he learned had been built of very ancient work by the faithful among the Romans, and consecrated it in the name of the holy Saviour, our God and Lord Jesus Christ; and he appointed this for a habitation for himself and for his successors'.

The second church was that already in use by Queen Bertha and her chaplain: it lay outside the Roman city walls, and it has been suggested that it was, in fact, a cemetery chapel or martyrium. Bede says that 'there was to the east of the city a church built of old in honour of St Martin while the Romans inhabited Britain, in which the queen, whom we have said to have been a Christian, was wont to pray'. St Martin actually died in 397, at a time when it was not the custom to dedicate churches to any saints except the apostles, or to martyrs whose bodies rested in the church. St Martin was the first West European saint not a martyr in whose name churches were dedicated; but even so, his basilica at Tours was known as the church of St Martin rather because his body lay there than by reason of a special act of dedication; it is considered impossible by experts that a church in Britain should have been dedicated in his name before the middle of the fifth century, within, that is, some fifty years of his death. St Martin was, however, the patron saint of the kings of Paris, and the Canterbury dedication may stem from some form of restoration and dedication by Liuthard; or, indeed, from the procuring of a relic and its laying up beneath an altar even before the days of Bertha and Liuthard. In any case, the old, Roman-built, church was one that Augustine must early have visited.

The third Roman church is not mentioned by Bede, but has been discovered by recent excavation. Since the bombing, various sites in Canterbury have been excavated before rebuilding, and the grid-plan and walls of Roman Canterbury have been established. It has been observed by Professor Sheppard Frere,[1] in charge of the excavations, than the plan of the modern church of St Peter lies at an angle to the medieval and modern road: but aligned, in fact, to the old Roman street. It must have been repaired, or rebuilt, in such a way as to preserve continuity with the old Roman church site.

Durovernum, as Augustine saw it, would have looked to us a shanty town. The houses of the Roman city had been built in their own grounds, as at Silchester, and not strictly and continuously aligned to the street, as at Caerwent; Durovernum has been said 'to have belonged to the garden city type' of Roman town. How much of it remained in Augustine's day?

Something remained. The roads were of hard, rammed gravel, and so was the floor of the Forum. The great theatre was at first an earthen declivity on which wooden seats were banked, but about A.D. 200 it was rebuilt with seating supported on massive vaulted masonry; the foundations of the circular colonnade still exist, but much more of the stone work would have remained in Augustine's day. The houses had been built with walls of timbering and hard mortar, with sometimes a second story of half timbered work; the finest work in the houses were the floors of mosaic or coloured tiles. The internal walls had been of flint, or of timber and plaster, or clay. The basilica had once been lined with thin marble slabs, coloured

[1] Prof. Sheppard Frere very kindly told the writer this; see also his *Roman Canterbury,* a 'non-technical summary written by the archaeologist in charge of the Excavations 1945–1957'. Eastern Canterbury has been most excavated, because most heavily bombed in the war: the rectangular grid plan of Durovernum was discovered.

marbles brought from Egypt or Algeria, Italy or Thessaly. But none of these buildings, apart from the masonry of the theatre, were of massive, stone structure—unless the churches and the basilica were of stone.

It seems that at no time after the collapse of Roman rule was the city left deserted and in ruins: inhabitation in some form was continuous, as the pottery and a few coins from the rubbish pits show: but the Cantware settlers did not take over the Roman town intact and live in the Roman houses.[1] Some fell into ruin and the new inhabitants used their material and roofing to make houses of their own. The old grid-iron plan was lost already by Augustine's day; the Watling Street running through the town to cross the river from south to north remained, the roads from Richborough, Lympne and Reculver, fortresses that had once defended Durovernum, remained, but, for the rest, the Cantware had built themselves houses as suited themselves and the new track ways that crossed the city. Their houses lay across the old Roman streets: flimsy structures easily disturbed by later pits, cellars and new building. To one or a number of these, either inside the city walls, or near the church of St Martin, Augustine led his monks and interpreters. Here he must settle, to live and convert the king and such candidates for baptism as came to him; here he must, when he should be bishop, train an episcopal *familia* to be his clergy.

Bede's description of the ordering of Augustine's household in his new dwelling is of interest. He says that as soon as Augustine settled in his dwelling, 'he began to imitate the apostolic life of the primitive church, in continual prayers, fastings and vigils, in preaching the word of life to those he could, by despising all worldly things as strangers and pilgrims, by receiving from those they taught only the necessary food, by living in all things prepared to suffer adversity or even to die for those things which they preached, by being steadfast in the truth. Why do I delay then? Some believed and were baptised, marvelling at the simplicity and innocence of their life and the sweetness of the heavenly doctrine they preached.'

The new church of the Saviour was not yet restored; so they began, says Bede, to use the queen's church of St Martin's. He

[1] See Sheppard Frere, *ibid.* p. 18

says nothing of Liuthard, sent with the queen so many years ago, and the absence of any reference to him suggests that he was dead. In this church they first assembled, sang psalms, prayed, celebrated the mass, preached and baptised. Bede wrote before Charlemagne and Benedict of Aniane had prescribed a manner of life for monks and those priests later called 'canons', because they lived a life more or less according to the canons of a certain Chrodegang, bishop of Metz, who had died in 766. Bede wrote before the council of 817 differentiated between the *vita canonica*, lived by clergy in community under bishop or *praepositus*, and the old, half-communal life lived by the young clerks in training under a bishop, together with certain of the bishop's deacons, who might be retained for some years in that status to write his letters and conduct his business affairs. Bede, that is, had never heard of 'canons', and he is here describing loosely the ideal and apostolic life of a bishop's *familia*.

Since Augustine had now been received into Æthelberht's capital and given a permanent dwelling, it was fitting that he should fulfil the pope's intention of getting himself consecrated bishop, for it was fitting that a bishop should pour upon the king the waters of baptism. Bede states that in 597, the year after his arrival, Augustine made his way to Arles; Vergilius was there metropolitan bishop, and it was from him that Augustine must have received consecration, though Bede once confuses another bishop with him.

Augustine was already a bishop in 597 as is shown by Gregory's calling him 'his co-bishop' in a letter to Queen Brunhild. That Augustine should have travelled for consecration to so distant a bishop as the metropolitan of Arles has been questioned, and it has been suggested that he was, in fact, consecrated at Autun by Bishop Syagrius, Brunhild's supporter and counsellor. The journey to Autun was about half as long as that to Arles, it is true, and Gregory in a later letter speaks of Syagrius as having shown kindness to Augustine; but Gregory at the time had his doubts about Syagrius as having been involved in a movement of doubtful orthodoxy. In this very letter when he speaks of Augustine as already bishop, he refused Brunhild's request for the sending of a pallium to Syagrius, and sent it instead to the priest Candidus, rector of the patrimony in Gaul.

It seems rather that Bede was right in speaking of Augustine's consecration as having taken place at Arles. He was relating what he had heard from Canterbury: the fact and place of the consecration were important, and likely to be recorded. Even before the church at Canterbury had begun to keep an Easter table, a list of the consecrations and obits of the bishops of the see would be kept, according to custom, as the first and most important record of the see.

Nor is Arles as a place of consecration unlikely. The notaries of the *scrinium* had an old notitia of the provinces, cities and mother cities of the Gauls, and Arles ranked in such a notitia as the mother city of the whole prefecture (after the withdrawal of the capital from Trier). More than one record suggests that Pope Gregory and the Roman *scrinium* were better acquainted with the administrative divisions of the later Roman empire than with the contemporary political situation in the lands of the Franks and the Anglo-Saxons. Gregory later ordered Augustine to have his metropolitical see at Londinium: Paulinus baptised Edwin at Eboracum, which was not Edwin's capital. Moreover, Gregory's later letters show that he was careful to define Augustine's relations with the Frankish bishops. He may well have considered Augustine's consecration by the metropolitan of Arles to be the correct canonical procedure, such as would establish his position with the utmost regularity.

On his return, Augustine and his interpreters continued the work of preaching the faith to the king and to such of his subjects as were willing to receive baptism. Bede says that the baptisms took place at St Martins; and as no mention is made of a baptistery there, nor has any trace been found of a church of this period with a separate baptistery, the baptisms must, it would seem, have been made in the kind of late Roman shallow tank which has been found by excavation at more than one place in Britain. These shallow leaden baths, with sides about a foot high, have the alpha and omega sign on the sides; they mark a kind of transitional stage between the stone Roman bath, down into which the candidate for baptism stepped, and the deep medieval font, raised on a pillar, into which the priest lowered the naked infant; the word 'font' itself, of course, means originally 'spring'. The use of such a low, leaden bath,

inscribed on the side with holy symbols, accords with the contemporary description of candidates who 'entered the waters of
baptism'.

And when he [the king] himself, with others, was pleased with
their pure and holy life, and the sweetness of their promises, which
were attested by the showing of many miracles, he believed and
was baptised, and many began daily to flock to hear the word of
God, and to leave their pagan religion and by faith to unite themselves with the holy church of Christ. For the king showed himself pleased with their faith and conversion but he did not compel
any man to be a Christian, but rather, he loved the believers more
fervently as fellow citizens of the heavenly kingdom. For he
learned from his teachers and the authors of his salvation that the
service of Christ should be voluntary, not an enforced servitude.
Nor did he delay in granting to his teachers the place of a see,
suitable to their rank, in his metropolitan city of Durovernum,
and at the same time to confer on them necessary possessions of
all kinds.[1]

'The place of a see' signifies the old ruined church which
should receive Augustine's chair, his seat, his cathedra: the
outward sign of his apostolic office of preaching. To this old
Roman church which Augustine restored as the church of the
Saviour he transferred the saying of office by the monks of his
familia, the celebration of the vigils before Sundays and feast
days, the mass that was the culmination of the vigil, the
exhortation and teaching by himself and the one or two priests
he had with him, and the baptismal laver. On this site the
present cathedral of Christ Church has grown during the
centuries, and it has not been possible to discover by excavation
the walls of Augustine's church, as he used it. Excavation has
shown however that its site, and that of Augustine's *mansio*,
were, in the main, thinly built over part of the Roman
Durovernum.

There is no record or suggestion that Augustine's forty
monks were ever transferred, as a body, from the monastic to
the clerical order; yet they acted, from the time of his consecration, as his episcopal *familia*. They had, in fact, the tonsure,
and Augustine as bishop could, if he thought a monk sufficiently
literate, raise him to any grade of the clerical order, and finally

[1] Plummer, I, p. 47

ordain him priest. It is unlikely that he so raised many monks, but we hear of his sending Lawrence the priest and Peter the monk to Gregory in 597, to bear witness of his consecration, and this Lawrence was later to succeed him as archbishop of Canterbury. The fact that Augustine appealed to Gregory for more helpers suggests that he had few monks of the original mission whom he could raise to the priesthood. The chief hope for the future lay in the boys whom he hoped to be given him, to be trained for long years in his *familia* and receive the priesthood at thirty or forty years of age. The monks whom he had brought would, when they had learned to some extent the English language, help teach these boys, do the domestic work of the house and the sacristan work of the church, chant the office, care for the sick and guests (all bishops of the day had a guest-house or xenodochium), and prepare the church for the baptisms and the eucharist. The direct instruction of catechumens would be left to Augustine and his priest or priests. They would still be monks: though the boys in training would be young clerks, and it is doubtful if monastic postulants would be received before Augustine's new monastery of SS Peter and Paul could be built. For many years Augustine's *familia* would have been described as monks, though an increasing number of them could be described as clergy; they lived in community, in obedience to Augustine, and in the two centuries of the mixed rule that were still to run before Charlemagne's ordinances, no one would have found their position anomalous.

The date of Æthelberht's baptism, though implied by Bede as preceding Augustine's consecration at Arles in 597, has recently been questioned. Though it was not papal practice to send a bishop on a precarious mission whose permanence was doubtful, yet it is likely that once a permanent foundation for a see had been made and a royal licence to teach granted, the baptism of the *bretwalda* would seem to demand the honourable and apostolic status of bishop for him who administered the sacrament. Moreover, a papal letter to Eulogios, patriarch of Alexandria, in July 598, though it is filled with rejoicing that so many English have received the faith, makes no mention of a royal baptism: 'the English,' said Gregory, 'who being placed in a remote corner of the world, have long bowed down to wood and stone', have through Eulogios's prayers been converted.

No mention is however made of King Æthelberht's conversion, though this in the situation of the day was all important and a guarantee of success. In 601, however, Queen Bertha was exhorted by letter to continue her efforts for the king's spiritual progress; and in that same month Gregory wrote formally to Æthelberht exhorting him to be another Constantine and convert his people. He must just have heard from the messengers sent by Augustine of the king's baptism.

At some time before June 601, then, King Æthelberht entered the waters of baptism. According to custom, he would have been received during the long ceremonies of the Easter or Pentecost vigil. Water mingled with the chrism would have been poured on him as he stood in the baptismal font, and the cross signed on his forehead. For Augustine, when the long ceremonies ended in the Alleluia of the mass, it was the sure pledge that the souls of the English would now be saved, a sign that Christ had indeed risen and appeared unto Peter; Æthelberht, risking his earthly kingdom, would one day gain the shores of the heavenly kingdom. For the historian, it marks also the point when the waters of the Tiber began to flow into the Kentish Stour, and a Mediterranean civilisation to influence a Germanic society.

## CHAPTER 3

# The Sending of Fresh Helpers in 601

AUGUSTINE was now a bishop and he had made many converts: Pope Gregory told the patriarch Eulogios that many thousands had been received to baptism at the first Christmas after his arrival in 597. But it is clear that his band of monks, some of them the oblate youths bought in the slave market, was lacking in priests capable of episcopacy and able to lay the foundations of the church in a pagan and largely hostile land. Gregory sent to Rome for fresh helpers, and together with this appeal a number of queries about his future dispositions for the English church.

Bede's dating of this appeal is somewhat difficult to reconcile with the length of time before Gregory answered it. Bede says he sent it immediately after his return from consecration at Arles: 'Returning to Britain he [Augustine] forthwith [*continuo*] sent to Rome Lawrence the priest and Peter the monk, to tell Pope Gregory that the English people had received the faith of Christ and that he had been made a bishop.' Apparently Bede had written this before he received from Canterbury the copies of Gregory's letters to various people showing that the helpers were sent by Gregory not before July 601; he inserted the text of the letters into his history, without altering his earlier statement that Augustine had returned from Arles and sent the appeal '*continuo*'. It would seem possible that Æthelberht had been baptised in the early summer of 601, and the appeal sent when it was now clear that the English would need more bishops to preach the faith to the kings of the sub-kingdoms adjacent to the Cantware: to the men of west Kent and to the East Saxons.

Bede saw fit to insert before his account of Augustine's appeal to Rome a long tract consisting of his queries and Gregory's answers, undated (see p. 61n.). Then he recounted how Augustine the bishop had suggested to Gregory that the harvest stretching before him in England was indeed great, but the labourers few, and how the pope had then sent to him together with his official embassy many helpers and ministers of the word, among whom the first and most eminent were Mellitus, Justus, Paulinus and Rufinianus. With them he sent all things necessary for the worship and ministry of the church, namely sacred vessels and altar vestments, and also ornaments for churches, and priestly and clerical garments, and relics of the saints and martyrs (for laying up beneath the new altars), together with very many books. And he sent also a letter, in which he intimated that he had sent Augustine a pallium, and told him also in what manner he ought to appoint bishops in Britain. And this is the text of the letter:

> To our most reverend and holy brother Augustine, our co-bishop, Gregory, servant of the servants of God:
> Since it is certain that ineffable rewards in the eternal kingdom are reserved for those who labour for almighty God, still it is needful for us also to award a tribute of honour, that they should toil the more zealously through a more ample reward. And because the new church of the English has, through the Lord's help and your labours, been brought to the grace of God, we grant to you the use of the pallium, to be used only in the performance of the solemnities of holy mass. And also that in twelve separate places you shall ordain bishops who shall be subject to your rule, so that the bishop of the city of Londinium ever for the future shall be consecrated by his own synod, and receive the honour of the pallium from this holy and apostolic see which, by the ordinance of God, I serve.

It is notable that, following the ancient metropolitan disposition of the province of southern Britain in Roman times, Gregory set Augustine's see in the old metropolis, Londinium, regardless of the fact that the place for a see had already been given by the *bretwalda* to Augustine, and that Londinium was now the capital of the relatively small sub-kingdom of the East Saxons. The messengers from Canterbury to Bede made no comment on the fact that Augustine's see had never in the intervening century and more, been moved from Canterbury to London. Such a papal designation and re-establishment of an old Roman metropolitan see, never in fact realised in that place, can be paralleled by continental examples. Augustine's see remained in Canterbury (see p. 58).

But to the city of Eboracum (the old capital of the northern province) we wish also that you should send a bishop, him whom you yourself shall see fit to ordain; so that if that same city with its neighbouring regions shall receive the word of God, he also shall ordain twelve bishops and enjoy metropolitan honour; for we dispose, if he in his life be a fit companion to you in yours, to award to him also the pallium, by the grace of God: and yet nevertheless our will is to subject him to your disposition. But after his death he shall preside over the bishops that he shall ordain without being in any way subject to the bishop of Londinium.

In future, however, there shall be this distinction of honour between the bishops of the city of Eboracum and of Londinium; that he shall be held the senior who was ordained first to his see; those matters which ought to be done out of zeal for Christ they shall arrange and do unanimously; let them decide aright, and let them carry out what they decide without disagreement between themselves.

The pope then concluded his letter, the foundation document for the setting up of the provinces of Canterbury and York, with a paragraph showing that he was aware of the existence of Celtic bishops in Britain. They existed in fact in the western and northern borders of Britain, where the old Roman rule had been relatively weak, but which the Anglo-Saxon invaders reached later or not at all. Between them and the Mediterranean there were few sea traders or pilgrims. Gregory knew very little about the Celtic Christians and their bishops: what little he knew probably came from information brought by Augustine's messengers rather than from any independent source. When he had sent off Augustine from Rome in 596, it is unlikely that he knew anything about them at all; if, as the evidence of his commendatory letters suggests, he didn't know the name of any bishop north of Tours, it is unlikely that he knew anything of bishops beyond the Channel. But it is notable that in setting up the provincial structure of the English church, he did know that somewhere, beyond the *bretwalda*-ship of Æthelberht, there were bishops of the Britons: and the Britons were the still unsubdued enemies of the Anglo-Saxons and of Æthelberht. Gregory could not make any detailed arrangements about these

Celtic bishops or even communicate with them. The remarkable thing is that he had no doubt they were bishops, if somewhat outlandish and uninstructed of life. He concluded his letter:

> And you, my brother, shall through the grace of our Lord Jesus Christ have subject to you not only those bishops whom you yourself have ordained, and not only those ordained by the bishop of Eboracum, but even all the bishops [*sacerdotes*: at the time meaning bishops] of Britain; so that they may learn from the teaching and life of your holiness both the rule of right faith and the pattern of a good life, so that they may execute their office with the right faith and manner of life and when God shall will, attain to the heavenly kingdom. May God keep you, most reverend brother.

Bede's history, and the text of Gregory's letters preserved in his Register, throw more light on the sending of this second mission, whose safe passage to Britain the pope tried to further by more letters of commendation. Some of the letters, enrolled by the notaries of the *scrinium*, are dated as written in June 601, some in July 601; it is clear that in these months Gregory was conferring with the messengers sent by Augustine and debating with himself the decisions he should make, but all the letters were kept till they could be taken back through Gaul by Gregory's new band of helpers. It is also clear from other letters in the Register that the pope knew that he would be sending a large body of clergy and their assistants northward through Gaul; he prepared, therefore, other letters to Frankish clerics for the settlement of any other business he had on hand.

The commendatory letters written by Gregory included one to the old queen Brunhild and another to her enemy, King Lothar II, the son of Chilperic and Fredegond. Fredegond herself had died in 597, and the young king Lothar II exercised a small and shadowy power in Normandy (Neustria). The pope thanked Lothar for help given earlier to Augustine and his monks, as had been reported to him by Lawrence the priest and Mellitus the abbot, who were then returning again to Augustine in Kent. A 'blanket' letter commending Lawrence the priest, Mellitus the abbot and the monks with them was prepared by the notaries for delivery to the bishops Serenus of Massilia, Lupus of Chalons-sur-Saône, the bishop of Toulon-sur-Arroux, Simplicius of Paris, Licinius of Angers, and Melantius of Rouen. Another June letter to Desiderius, bishop of Vienne, commended to him the persons of Lawrence and Mellitus, now travelling back to Bishop Augustine. A letter to Bishop Vergilius of Arles commended to him the monks he was sending to Bishop Augustine, and bade him hold a synod to deal with the matter of simony: he has heard that a price is demanded for the conferring of orders. Another letter to Vergilius, quoted by Bede and apparently sent at the same time, suggests to Vergilius that, if it happen that 'our common brother, Augustine the bishop' come to him, Vergilius should welcome him with love and receive his admonitions: for it often happens that others at a distance get to know of things that should be emended before those on the spot; 'let him hold an inquiry to clear the innocent and punish the guilty'. There is no evidence, however, that Augustine ever made another journey to Arles; though other letters of Gregory confirm his belief that certain abuses existed in the church of the Franks. He did, in fact, write in June 601 to Queen Brunhild, lamenting that he has heard from the accounts given him by many persons that the 'bishops of those parts live evilly and impudently': he asked her permission to send a legate, to hold a synod with other bishops and inquire into these misdoings. This same month, June 601, Gregory wrote yet a third letter to Brunhild, commending Lawrence and Mellitus, and specifying that the abuse of simony exists among the Frankish priests. He wrote also to Theoderic (Thierry), king of the Franks, advising him to summon a synod to deal with simony, and thanking him for help earlier given to Augustine and his monks; some of these monks have returned to him in Rome and told him of Theoderic's kindness; they are now returning to Bishop Augustine and he commends them to the king.

The adherent of highest standing who had volunteered to serve under Bishop Augustine, and who was later ordained by him as bishop of London, a dangerous and precarious post, was 'Mellitus the abbot from the Gauls' (*ex Gallicis*). It is of interest that he was a monk, and one whose natural speech, as Frankish, would be nearer to that of the English than the liquescent Latin spoken by the Romans. If Gregory had sent Frankish 'interpreters' along with Augustine, here was an abbot who would get the hang of English speech as well as they. As destined for a bishop's see, he would have to deal with pagan sanctuaries, 'temples', 'fanes'; and Gregory wrote him some words of advice:

> To my beloved son, Mellitus the abbot, Gregory, the servant of the servants of God.
>
> After the departure of our congregation which is accompanying you, we have been in suspense, for we have not happened to hear any word about the prosperity of your journey. But when Almighty God shall lead you to our most reverend brother, Augustine the bishop, tell him what I have long been debating within myself about English matters; namely, that the temples of idols among that people ought by no means to be destroyed, though the idols that are in them ought to be destroyed. Let water be blessed and sprinkled in these fanes, and let altars be set up and relics placed in them. And let them set up for themselves bowers built of the branches of trees around these new churches now changed from what used to be of old fanes; and let the solemn day be celebrated with religious feasting. Let them not sacrifice animals to devils, but let them kill animals for their own eating, to the praise of God, and give thanks to the giver of all things that their hunger is satisfied, so that while certain external joys are preserved for them, they may the more easily be led on to the joys that are within. For doubtless it is impossible to cut off everything at once from those slow of understanding, and such people who can only ascend to the highest by footsteps, a little at a time; they cannot, indeed, be raised up by leaps and bounds.

Gregory had insured, as far as he could, the safety of the second band of missionaries he was sending to England, and he sent also letters to the principal characters involved in what one might call the Kentish mystery play: Augustine and Æthelberht and Queen Bertha. The letter to Augustine about the setting up of metropolitan sees in Londinium and Eboracum had been official, sent out by the *scrinium*, in correct diplomatic form, duly dated by the day, month and year of the East Roman emperor Maurice, and by the indiction. But Gregory sent also to Augustine a personal letter, perhaps entrusted directly to Augustine's messengers, for it has come down to us without the formal diplomatic beginning and ending: a letter of spiritual advice. In it Gregory warned his 'dearest brother' against spiritual pride in his achievement and particularly against glorying in the miracles God had worked at his hands in the course of the mission; since they had been worked for the sake of converting souls, not for the praise of Augustine, let him distrust himself, and remember that the Lord bade his disciples rejoice, not because the devils were subject to them, but for that their names were written in heaven.

To Queen Bertha Gregory wrote, in a letter unquoted by Bede, praising her for her devotion, bidding her encourage her husband in his progress in the faith, and sending her presents.

To Æthelberht, 'his son', he wrote, with the correct diplomatic beginning and ending, as befitted a letter addressed to the 'king of the English', that he had heard of what Æthelberht had done among the people of the English, and how his subjects had gained heavenly benefits through the king' spower and goodwill. 'And therefore, O my glorious son,' he continued, 'cherish the grace you have been divinely given, and hasten to extend the Christian faith among your subjects.' He should increase his zeal for their conversion, exterminate the worship of idols, overturn their fanes, build up good customs and the good life among his subjects by all means, and win for himself a heavenly reward. Moreover, he recalled to Æthelberht the example of the great emperor Constantine, who withdrew the whole Roman republic from the worship of idols: let Æthelberht be another Constantine. Let him hear the teaching of 'our most reverend brother, Augustine the bishop, who is well taught in monastic rule and filled with the knowledge of holy scripture': let him hear, ponder, and carry out Augustine's words. 'The end of this world is approaching,' he wrote, 'and many signs confirm this: there are famines and pestilences and earthquakes in divers places: not all things shall come to pass in our days, but after our days all shall be fulfilled.' But let not the king be perturbed, for these signs of the world's ending are permitted that we may be prepared for the hour when the Judge cometh. 'We are sending you,' the pope concluded, 'small presents that will not seem small to you since they are sent you from blessed Peter the apostle. May God keep you.'

When Pope Gregory dictated this letter, on 22 June 601, he must certainly have heard of Æthelberht's conversion, as is shown by his comparison of the English king with the emperor Constantine.

Bede then relates Augustine's measures for the establishment of the Christian mission among the English (for the papal replies to Augustine's queries, see Chapter 5). He had now the papal instructions how to build up the structure of the future English Church, though he could scarcely hope to accomplish all this in his own life-time.

Æthelberht, it is true, was the *bretwalda*, and the position of *bretwalda* gave its holder the right to summon the kings of the smaller English kingdoms to follow him to battle; it was gained by victory in battle over those kings, or, at least, over those who were not willing to concede the position to the claimant without fighting. But it gave him no right whatever to interfere in the sub-kingdoms: to exact any revenue from them, intervene in the succession of their kings or in their domestic affairs. Æthelberht had been king for a long time in 597; there were, besides him, kings of the West Saxons, the East Saxons, the South Saxons, the East Angles and the northern Angles of Deira and Northumbria; there were also other tribal leaders. While Æthelberht was still a young king, two princes of the West Saxons, Ceawlin and Cutha, had fought against him and (the Anglo-Saxon Chronicle says) defeated him at Wimbledon, in 568. But the West Saxons were continually fighting against the Britons of Somerset and Gloucester, while the kingdom of Kent was prospering through the cross-Channel trade: at some time, the positions of Ceawlin and Æthelberht were reversed, and the latter became *bretwalda*. Æthelberht's dominance over the East Saxons, a less numerous people, was apparently secure because his sister Ricula had married Sledda, the East Saxon king. His interests were less directly involved with the more distant East Angles, and less involved still with the northern Angles. When the Anglo-Saxon Chronicle was put together, in King Alfred's reign, no record survived of any battles by which Æthelberht had gained the position of *bretwalda*: but some such there probably were; at any rate there is no doubt about Bede's listing him as the third of the seven Anglo-Saxon *bretwaldas*. He lived to be an old man, indeed he had the longest reign recorded of any Anglo-Saxon king; but his power was military, personal and precarious. It was certain to diminish in old age. Pope Gregory, writing at Rome in the home of the Roman emperors and with knowledge of Ostrogothic and

Visigothic kings, could not well understand Æthelberht's position, or how his power to favour Christian missionaries and
grant lands to maintain them was limited to his own kingdom
of Kent and possibly to the neighbouring kingdom of the East
Saxons, where his sister was or had been queen, and the king
his nephew.

Gregory could not well understand, either, the reality of the
Anglo-Saxon opposition to Christianity whether in Kent or and
among the East Saxons. These Germanic people had conquered and settled in south-east Britain without any general
intermingling of population with the conquered Britons, who
had been and were Christian. Kent had had some of the
finest villas of the Roman official class and a peasantry at least
nominally Christian: but there had been a great flight of
Christian Britons westward, and even across the Channel to
Armorica, which now gained the name of the lesser Britain, or
Brittany. Some conquered Romano-Britons did remain, even
in Kent, but they were a subject class, the Welsh, called 'læts'
by the invaders, and with a lesser wergeld than the free men,
who were all Anglo-Saxons or, as they were called locally, the
Cantware. The Cantware found ruins of pagan temples built
in early times by the Romans, but they built for themselves
hill sanctuaries and went on venerating their own gods, Woden
and Thor, whose names occur so often in southern English
place-names. To the Cantware and the East Saxons, Christianity was not only a foreign religion, but it was the religion of
their serfs, in so far as these serfs remembered religion at all. It
was the religion of the Welsh, always the enemies of the Saxons,
against whom they had so long fought and against whom they
were still fighting in the west and north. To accept Christianity was, to many among the Cantware, a national humiliat-
ion. What did they want with a Frankish religion, or a Welsh
religion? To many of the old conservatives this change of
religion that the king was so keen on was likely to be very
unlucky.

The reality of this Germanic, nationalist aversion to Christianity is seen by comparison with the fate of Christianity among
the middle Angles and in the north. Penda and his subjects,
the middle Angles, long remained pagan. In Northumbria and
Deira the conquering Angles were few: they settled down,

ruled and lived among a Celtic population. Celtic ornament, scroll and interlace, prevailed over their own Germanic ornament, in stone and wood-carving and in metalwork. Later ornament in the Bewcastle cross or the Lindisfarne gospels was Celtic, not Germanic. No such Celtic scrolls survive to us from early days in Kent; Æthelberht had some very fine brooches made by his own goldsmiths, but the design was Germanic, like that of the East Anglian ornaments at Sutton Hoo. The Celtic population of Northumbria and Deira may well have forgotten their Christianity in the sixth and early seventh centuries, when the new missionaries came, but they were of the same stock as the Celts across the Irish Sea and the Celts and Picts north of Hadrian's Wall, who were Christian: they had no nationalist aversion to a religion that was already held by the greater part of the people of their own race. They were not conscious that their ancestors had always venerated Woden and Thor. King Edwin of Deira had, of course, his own pagan, Germanic sanctuary at Goodmanham, but its priest was less than lukewarm (see p. 114).

In view of the nationalist instincts of the Anglo-Saxon south, including the kingdom of Kent, Augustine's difficulties and the limitation to the spread of his mission can be understood. Æthelberht and Bertha were, by 601, getting old; Æthelberht lived till 616, and, when Bertha died before him, married again, but his power waned with his physical vigour. The conversion of the Cantware depended almost entirely on his personal will.

Augustine in 601 was living in the *mansio* given him by the king. This was probably an *aula* or hall such as the Cantware would have built for their king, either within the walls of Durovernum or outside. The upper storeys of Roman Durovernum had been of wood, and it is perhaps, to be guessed that these Kentish 'halls' were of wood also, for the Anglo-Saxons were used to building in wood, as witness the rectangular 'halls' for king and nobles recently excavated at Yeavering, north of Hadrian's Wall. On the other hand, there was plenty of hewn stone available for building in post-Roman Durovernum. It is unlikely that archaeological evidence of the king's, or Augustine's, hall will ever be found, for there has been too much disturbance and rebuilding of medieval Canterbury for

post-holes now to be discovered; these would have enabled the
plan of a wooden building to be traced. Augustine's *aula* is
considered likely to have been of wood and near to his see
church. The see church would probably, as at Silchester, and
in the case of so many small Roman temples, have been either a
basilica with aisles, or a simple rectangular chamber, with an
apse at one or both ends. No trace of work of Augustine's
period has been discovered at Christ Church, which is
undoubtedly built over and around Augustine's 'church of the
Saviour'; but a description of the church before its destruction
by fire in 1067 contains just a hint as to the form of Augustine's
church, if the description be considered in conjunction with
the church of St Augustine's monastery, which he undoubtedly
planned. The description itself appears to be that of Christ
Church as rebuilt by Archbishop Odo (940–60), but when it
says that the church had an *aula*, with aisles and two towers
halfway down and above the aisles, it would seem likely that
Augustine's church was only half the length of Odo's, and that
the towers over Odo's aisles were originally the roofs over
the two *porticus* of a cruciform church. The east end of
Augustine's church would have been apsidal, and level with,
or only a step raised above, the nave. The making of a *confessio* or chamber for relics would have been later than
Augustine's time and more consonant with the age of Wilfrid,
who brought back relics for an underground crypt at Hexham,
and possibly at Wing, in Buckinghamshire. The raising of the
high altar on steps above the *confessio* would also have been
much later than Augustine's time. The dedication of altars in
the two 'towers' of bishop Odo's day, the northern one to St
Gregory and the southern one to St Augustine, supports the
conjecture that they were indeed built over what had been the
*porticus* of St Augustine's church.

Here, as soon as the church was built, the clergy and monks
of Augustine's *familia* would say the office, and admit the king
and the Christian nobles and people to preachings and baptisms. No great numbers could be assembled, for the church was
small; and though a standing congregation can be packed very
tight, for instance at the great feasts, yet many must have been
left to listen to the chanting from outside, if the thousands
whom Bede says Augustine baptised tried to assemble, as for

the Easter feast. Here Augustine broke the 'fair and comely loaf' (*panem nitidem*) at the mass and gave communion to Æthelberht and the converts: here he blessed the wine brought from France, which the queen knew should be supplied to him. She remembered that Bishop Liuthard had had special coins minted with his name on them, to buy the wine brought by the Frankish merchants, for King Æthelberht never troubled to have any coins made; he said he had never met a merchant who refused to take a shaling or shilling (a slice cut from his golden bangle). She had told him she thought these shalings or shillings very rustic and old-fashioned and that, moreover, she liked to have a proper coin for her Easter offering; but the king only laughed and said Frankish coins were not too hard to get. Bishop Augustine had, of course, to have wine for the mass, so Bertha saved up Frankish coins to buy wine for him.

When Augustine had built the church of the Saviour and received from the king and certain nobles boys to train as the clergy of an episcopal *familia*, he was not yet content. He still had many monks with him, men too simple or too old to be trained for the priesthood and pastoral work, and he wished to provide for them. At Rome, moreover, and this was true of other Italian cities, though the great basilicas had small monasteries attached to them for monks to pray, day and night, before the bodies of the holy apostles and martyrs, yet the monks were never themselves the bishop's *familia*, conducting all the bishop's pastoral and legal business. It would be well to separate his own monks from his clergy, and to build a monastery for them under an abbot. He besought the king to give him the place where the *vita monachica* could be led as he had known it *ad clivum Scauri*, and at length he got the royal assent.

'It would be well,' he said to the king, 'that a church should be built within a monastery where the kings of Kent might be afforded royal burial, and he himself and all the bishops of Durovernum might lie when their time came. For the bodies of your ancestors,' he said, 'were laid on the deck of a ship and the ropes tying her to the shore loosed when the wind blew from the shore, so that the ship sailed off upon the whale-path and was never seen again, or so I have been told: but men believed,' Augustine said, 'that she sailed to the land of the gods, which, as you know, cannot be true, for there are no such gods. Or else their bodies were burnt on a high pyre of flame, heathen sacrifices being offered. And this too you know to be no funeral rite for a Christian.'

The king looked uneasy and regretful. 'The flames blazed high for King Eormanric my father,' he said. 'I remember that we killed five oxen.'

'Exactly,' said Augustine. 'But the Christian burial rite, in a great church, is much finer: for the king's body rests in the church on a stretcher, as in life, brooch on shoulder and girt with sword belt; the bishop in the mass prays that Christ will receive his soldier to the heavenly banquet. All the night before, the monks pray; and the people pray with wails of supplication. And after the mass, the body is placed in a fine stone tomb in the *porticus* of the church, and oxen are killed, and the poor are fed in a great funeral feast. To feed the poor is a most Christian act. Indeed, all that come to pray for the king shall be fed at that feast. The stone tomb, with the king's name upon it, remains for ever, and the monks pray beside it in the church, day and night, till the Lord comes.'

'And if I make such a church,' Æthelberht asked, 'shall I then sleep there till he comes?'

'Your body indeed shall sleep there,' Augustine said, 'when God receives you to the heavenly kingdom; even so the kings of Paris sleep in the church of the holy martyr, St Denis. It is fitting that a Christian king should lie in such a church. But we do not know the day or hour when the Lord comes. Indeed, he said he would come as a thief in the night.'

'If he comes soon,' said Æthelberht, 'it is hardly worth while to build such a church, which would cost much money, and more land to feed the monks. Do you think he will come soon?'

'Our father Gregory has said to me that indeed he will come soon,' Augustine replied, 'for the Lombard armies were marching towards Rome and there were plagues, pestilences and famines, and men saw signs in the sky; all these things are signs of his coming. But since then summer and winter have come and gone many times, and the Lord has delayed his coming. Myself, I think he will not come yet; also, our father Gregory has written to me enjoining that many bishops' sees be set up; he too must have doubts now about the Lord's coming soon.'

'To set up many bishops' sees will take many years,' said Æthelberht, 'it will be better to have a burial church, perhaps.'

'Far better for you to sleep in such a church than in a heathen burial mound,' said the bishop.

'I suppose so,' said the king. 'A warrior cannot fight for two chieftains, and now I am Christ's soldier, it would be more fitting for me to sleep in a church than under even a high burial mound. I do not wish to appear inconstant, for then I shall be rejected both by Christ and Thor. Let it be a fine church, in this monastery of yours.'

'I will see about it,' said Augustine.

Then the king gave Augustine the place for a monastery, not far from the city to the east, and he ordered a church to be built, allowing it to be dedicated, as his bishop wished, to the blessed apostles, SS Peter and Paul. For the popes had sent relics of these saints, small cloths laid all one night against the tomb of St Peter in his basilica on the Vatican mount, and of St Paul in his basilica on the road to Ostia, and Augustine prepared to have them laid beneath the altar of the church of his new monastery. The church was planned as a large chamber with an apse for the altar at its end and a narthex to the west; beside the nave, a northern and a southern *porticus* were built to receive the tombs of the bishops of the Cantware, and their kings, respectively. The building was not finished before Augustine's death, so that its consecration fell to Lawrence, his successor: the church seems to have been finished by 613.

Now the first abbot of this monastery, Bede tells us, was that Peter who had been sent in 601 with Lawrence to Rome. He was made a priest and given charge of the monastery, whether before or after the consecration of the church is not known. The records of the council of Paris, 614, show that an 'abbas de Doroverno' attended, and it may have been this abbot Peter who attended. In any case, Bede states that Peter, abbot of SS Peter and Paul, was sent on a mission to Gaul, and was drowned in a bay called Amfleat (Ambleteuse) near Boulogne. The inhabitants, ignorant of his name and standing, buried the body simply and without honour; but a heavenly light shone at night above the place of his burial, till those who remarked it suspected that they had buried a saint; and they sought to find out who he was, and then buried him with suitable honour in a church in Boulogne.

Three years after Augustine had received his helpers from Rome in 601, when these had learned something of the Cantware and when Augustine had been able to persuade Æthelberht to use his position to urge the conversion of the East Saxons and the men of West Kent, he ordained two new bishops. Mellitus, the Gallic abbot, he ordained to the see of Londinium, for the East Saxons, who were separated from the Cantware by the river Thames. Londinium was a most important city, a great market for traders who came to it by land and sea. Æthelberht's nephew, Saeberht, reigned there. Mellitus could well understand the Frankish traders, and he could better understand the Saxons than an Italian would have done. Here again, however, though Æthelberht had persuaded the Saxon king to be converted, there was much opposition; the queen was steadfastly pagan and disdained her husband's meek acceptance of the rite of baptism. King Æthelberht himself, however, built in Londinium a see church for Mellitus and his successors, and Mellitus dedicated it to St Paul.

The chief city of the men of west Kent, Bede says, was the old Roman Durobrevis, about twenty-four miles to the west of Canterbury, which the English had called Rochester, from a chieftain of the earliest days of the invasion called Hrof. In this city Augustine, in 604, ordained Justus to be bishop and his successors after him. Æthelberht built him a see church, dedicated to St Andrew; he gave many gifts both to this church and that of Durovernum, together with lands and possessions for the use of the clergy who lived with the bishops.

'And at length' (in 604), says Bede, 'our beloved father Augustine died.' He was buried out of doors (for it was not yet lawful in Roman law to bury within a building), buried next the church of SS Peter and Paul, whose walls were rising, but which was not yet finished or dedicated. But as soon as the dedication was made, Augustine's body was borne inside, and buried as was fitting in the northern *porticus*, where indeed all the bodies of the succeeding archbishops were laid in tombs, all except those of Theodore and Berhtwald. Their bodies were placed within the church itself, because the aforesaid *porticus* could hold no more.

Now this *porticus* had in its midst an altar dedicated to St Gregory (for St Gregory had died, like Augustine, in 604, and cloths could be laid by his tomb and brought to Durovernum to be placed beneath this altar). At this altar on every Saturday a priest of the monastery solemnly celebrated the mass that ought to be celebrated on that day.

Now this epitaph is written on the tomb of Augustine:

'Here rests the Lord Augustine, the first archbishop of Durovernum, who was sent here in times past by blessed Gregory, pontiff of the city of Rome. Supported through God's help by the working of miracles, he led Æthelberht the king and his people from the worship of idols to faith in Christ, and having fulfilled the days of his office in peace, he died on the seventh kalends of June in the reign of the same king' (26 May 604).

<br>

### FRONTISPIECE

The diagram reproduced as the frontispiece is taken from f.77 of the manuscript, written about 1414, of the Chronicle of Thomas of Elmham, monk of St Augustine's Canterbury, now MS. 1 in the library of Trinity Hall Cambridge. On it is shown the arrangement of the high altar at St Augustine's Canterbury with the shrines of St Augustine and some of the early archbishops and Saxon saints placed behind it in the apsidal presbytery. This portion of the church appears to have been screened off and was entered by two doors placed on either side of the high altar. The names of the shrines are as follows: Reading from left to right:—Jambertus (765–92), Nothelmus (735–9), Mildreda, abbess of Minster in Thanet, whose body was brought to St Augustine's in 1030, Deusdedit (655–64), Justus (624–7), Laurencius (604–19), Augustine(597–604) at the head of the apse, Mellitus (619–24), Honorius (627–53), Theodorus (668–90) Adrianus, abbot of St Augustine's (671–708), Brithwaldus (693–731), Tatwinus (731–4). A number of these saints, who were formerly buried in or near the *porticus* of St Gregory on the north side of the early Saxon church, were translated to the positions seen here in 1091. Altars are indicated on the diagram before the shrines of SS. Mildreda, Augustine and Adrianus.

Above the high altar is a figure of Christ in Majesty and two angels. Between the central figure and the angel on the left is the shrine of St Letardus, bishop, and chaplain to Queen Bercta wife of King Ethelbert of Kent. Below the Christ is the shrine of King Ethelbert and on either side are the books sent by Pope Gregory the Great to St Augustine. It is possible that the sixth-century Gospels in Corpus Christi Cambridge MS. 286 may have been one of these.

F. WORMALD

## CHAPTER 4

# Augustine's Queries and Gregory's Answers

WHEN Bede was writing his *Ecclesiastical History* or, more strictly, when he had nearly finished writing it, in 731, his friend Nothelm arrived from Canterbury, bringing additional documents and information. Nothelm was a priest of great learning and weight. He had been a member of a family that might, before the days of the Heptarchy, have raised the South Saxons to as great a position as that of the East Saxons, but things had not worked out like that. The South Saxons had some cross-Channel trade with Neustria: but they had no great port like Londinium. In a charter of about a hundred years after Augustine's day, a king Nothelm of the South Saxons had still been rich and powerful enough to grant his sister land to found a monastery. It is possible that Bede's friend Nothelm was his son or cousin, or that he belonged in some way to the South Saxon royal house. Boys of noble family received special training in monastic and episcopal families, and Bede's friend had received clerical training in the *familia* of the bishop of London. His abilities, and probably his descent, were well enough known to that learned old monk, Abbot Hadrian of St Augustine's monastery, for him to be summoned to Canterbury, briefed in the history of the foundation of the see, and given copies of the letters that had been accumulated there from the days of Augustine. Indeed, he had been sent to Rome to copy more letters, if he could find them, in the rolls of the *scrinium*. Moreover, he was told all that Hadrian and the Canterbury clergy could tell him of the oral traditions of the see: he could tell Bede stories handed down by 'the tradition of our ancestors' (*traditione maiorum nostrum*). 'Our ancestors', had lived in the Roman Durovernum, which had kept its Roman walls and was still a walled city, a stronghold; but it had, by Bede's time, become in common parlance Cantwarabyrig, Canterbury. (Not, of course, in official documents: the archbishop was still bishop of Durovernum Cantiacorum.)

When Nothelm travelled up to Jarrow in 731, on his historical mission, it was far from the first time that the monks of St Augustine, or their abbot, had been in touch with Bede's monastery of Jarrow. The founder of that monastery, Benedict Biscop, had been a friend of both Archbishop Theodore and the Neapolitan monk Hadrian whom he had brought with him to England. Benedict Biscop had ruled St Augustine's monastery himself for two years before Hadrian's knowledge of the English tongue and the situation in Kent was sufficient for him to take the responsibility of ruling St Augustine's himself. Benedict Biscop then went up north to make his twin foundations in Northumbria, but he often visited the Canterbury monastery of Abbot Hadrian on his journeys to and from the Continent. Hadrian must have learned from him of his promising young monk scholar, Bede, and between the two monasteries books and learned writings were certainly exchanged.

Ten years before Nothelm's visit Bede was in possession of a long tractate, a copy of certain queries sent by Augustine to Pope Gregory.[1] Letters of that day were sent written on sheets of papyrus, probably rolled up for easiness of transport. The bishop who received such letters would keep them loose in some box or chest. Among them, and most carefully cherished at Durovernum, were the answers Pope Gregory had sent to Augustine in 601, answers which were not enrolled on the papal registers (unless a roll of the register has been lost). It therefore seems possible that Gregory had written the answers down and given them into the hands of the English messengers with whom he had so many conferences in the months of June and July 601. The letters, as they have come down to us, have at any rate no formal opening or ending. At some point a copy was made of these Gregorian answers, in which each was headed: 'A question of Augustine', and the answer, 'Gregory answered'. Exactly how the loose sheets of the letters had been headed, we do not know; some of the letters may have had openings not copied by the scribe who made of them a continuous treatise. The tractate, before it reached Bede, had

---

[1] For all these queries and answers, and their provenance, see Deanesly and Grosjean, 'The Canterbury Edition of the Answers of Pope Gregory I to St. Augustine', *Jour. of Eccles. Hist.*, X (1959), 1–49. For Bede's insertion of them into the *Historia Ecclesiastica*, see Plummer's edition I, pp. 48–62.

acquired a preface stating that this was a letter of the blessed Pope Gregory to Augustine the bishop whom he sent to preach to the [Anglo-] Saxons: Gregory had received writings from Augustine at the hands of Lawrence the priest and Peter the monk.

There has been much dispute in the past about the historical character of this tractate and whether it was a genuine 'letter' of Pope Gregory or not, especially as it was not enrolled by the *scrinium,* and one section (about lawful marriage) could not possibly have been written by Gregory. The tractate occurs in many of the collections of canonical manuscripts, sometimes in the Bedan form, sometimes in a form rather different, arranged as 'chapters'. It is accepted now that the tractate was put together from letters mainly Gregorian, though the preface and the section about marriage are certainly later than Gregory's day.

The question is still open as to who put these queries and answers together in the form of 'chapters', which differs some-what from the form in which they are presented in Bede's version. The chapter, or capitular form, appears to be the earlier. The Bedan form appears in some canonical collections, though never in a manuscript earlier than those of the *Ecclesiastical History.* What is certain is that Bede quoted from the letter in which Gregory prescribed the manner of life of Augustine's cathedral clergy as early as 721, when he composed his prose *Life and Miracles of Saint Cuthbert*: the quotation bore upon the clerical-monastic life at Lindisfarne under Cuthbert, as similar to that of Augustine at Christ Church. It would seem that Bede already had the tractate with him then; and it may well be that some monk or cleric at Canterbury composed the tractate there, as a way of transmitting to Jarrow the contents of these loose Gregorian letters. Possibly Nothelm himself put the tractate together and took it up to Bede before the year 721: or possibly Jarrow had the tractate in an early form, transmitted by Benedict Biscop as of great interest to any scholarly community.

But the form in which Bede quotes the tractate in the *Ecclesiastical History* could not have been put together much earlier than 721, because its directions about canonical marriage belong to the period when there were discussions in Europe about this matter, and the council of Rome, 721, laid down certain rulings consonant with those of the tractate (see p. 69).

In general then, the queries and answers given by Bede in the *Ecclesiastical History* are historical records of the correspondence of Augustine and Gregory in the summer of 601. Taking the queries as given in Chapter xxvii of the first book of the *Ecclesiastical History,* Augustine asked:

FIRST: About bishops: what shall be their manner of life with their clergy? and about the offerings which the faithful make at the altar, into what portions should they be divided, and how ought the bishop to act in the church?

Augustine was seeking papal guidance about the management of his revenue, and the support of his *familia*. He was receiving certain renders, probably in food, from the estates Æthelberht had given him; he was receiving also the offerings of the faithful at the eucharist, and these might be in kind or in coined money, or in gold ornaments, especially from the nobles. Should these offerings be taken, he wanted to know, into the general episcopal revenue, and the clerical household therewith supported completely, or should the clergy, at any rate the higher clergy, have stipends (the Vulgate word for wages)? And if so, on what principle? Augustine was training clergy for his see; he was maintaining a guest-house for the poor and travellers; he was preparing to send out clergy on new missions; he had with him many monks who would never be promoted to holy orders. In western Europe and in the Mediterranean (as he knew, and as is clear elsewhere in Gregory's letters) bishops shared their revenue with their clergy in varying proportions. Augustine sought direction.

Gregory answered that holy scripture taught, and especially in St Paul's letters to Timothy, what kind of life should be led in the household of God. It was the custom of the holy see to direct bishops that all revenue (*stipendio*) ought to be divided into four parts: one for the bishop and his household and hospitality, another for the clergy, a third for the poor (the guest-house and alms), and a fourth for the repair of churches. 'But,' said Gregory, well aware that Augustine had as yet no senior clergy living in his see but outside his household, and that he had the old monks and the boy and young men clerics to care for and train, 'since your fraternity is instructed in monastic rules, and you ought not to live separately from your clergy in the church of the English . . . you ought to institute this manner of life which was that of our fathers in the early days of the church, in which no man said that he had anything of his own, but they had all things in common.'

Gregory was here quoting from Acts 4:32, and there is no need to infer that he also had in mind Augustine of Hippo's use of this text as basic in the rule he suggested in Letter 211 for his sister's community. The text was basic also to that bishop's defence of his own requirement that his clergy should live communally with him, without separate stipends. The example of Augustine of Hippo must have been well known to Gregory; and so must the passage in the preface of the old Rule of the Master (see p. 134) where the same text is cited as a scriptural justification for the communal life of monks. The text was indeed much quoted as vindicating communal life for those set apart for the service of God, monks or clergy. Such clergy, living communally, could not yet be called 'canons', for Augustine of Hippo had failed to get any general injunction by a council that all episcopal clergy should live communally, though he had advocated it. It was not till the time of Benedict of Aniane that the canons of a council made provisions for the rule of life (*regula Aquisgranensis*) of clergy living communally; and it is not till this time that such clergy should properly be called 'canons': their life was not yet 'canonical'. It is no more correct to call Augustine's household clergy 'canons' than to call them 'Benedictine monks'. Some of his household were monks and not clergy, some were monastic clergy; all led the communal life.

Gregory's intention in sending Augustine to England to teach the apostolic faith and institute the apostolic office of bishops, with duly trained and ordained clergy to aid the bishops, is shown in the second part of his answer to this same query of Augustine. 'If there are clerks outside holy orders,' he wrote, 'who cannot lead a celibate life, wives ought to be allowed to them and they should receive stipends and live outside the household; for we know that it was written of these same fathers of whom we have been speaking (in the Acts), that "they divided to each man according as each had need". And thought should be given and provision made about their stipends, that they be kept under ecclesiastical rule and live a good life and be present at the singing of psalms (the divine office), and by God's help preserve their heart and tongue free from all things unlawful. But about those living the common life and about allotting portions and showing hospitality and giving alms, what need is there for us to write to you? For all that is left over is to be assigned to pious and religious uses, the lord and master of all things teaching us: "Every thing that is left over, give as alms, and behold all things are clean to you".'

The English boys received by Augustine, that is, shall be trained alike; some will go on to deacons' and priests' orders, which they would not receive for many years—priests' orders perhaps at the age of forty; though Bede, more than a hundred years later, was made priest at the age of thirty. But long before they reached such an age certain of the English boys would have shown themselves unfit for much study and the celibate life, though they knew most of the psalms by heart and could even read. There is no reference in Gregory's letter to a formal questioning of such boys as to whether they wished to live outside the household and take wives, or go on in training for holy orders, though such a formal questioning is referred to in certain Frankish councils: but the freedom to ask to be allowed to marry is provided for. Augustine received children, not as monastic oblates, who would have no freedom to marry, but as young clerks to whom he gave the tonsure, as did the bishops in Gaul. He had, as yet, no monastery where the strict *vita monachica* could be lived.

SECOND: Augustine asked what he was to do about the liturgy, 'since the faith is one, and there are churches which have divers customs, so that there is one custom of saying mass in the holy Roman church and another in those of the Gauls?'

Gregory replied that Augustine knew well the custom of the Roman church; he remembers that custom in which he was brought up. 'But it is pleasing to me that in whatever church you find anything more pleasing to almighty God, whether in the Roman church or in that of the Gauls or of any other place, that you should carefully choose that, and in the church of the English now newly brought to the faith you should authorise and teach this custom, which you have collected out of many churches. For things are not to be loved because of the place they come from, but places are to be loved because of the good things they have produced. Choose then from each individual church whatever things are devout and religious and right, and bind them together as it were in a sheaf, and impose them as a custom in the minds of the English.'

Gregory's answer is often commended for its broadmindedness and wisdom, but it should be remembered that it would have occasioned no surprise to Augustine at the time, nor to any of the higher Roman clergy. Apart from the canon of the mass, which would at Rome be very old, and the general 'shape' of the liturgy for the eucharist, the 'custom of masses' varied (as Augustine knew well and would have seen in his long journeys through the Gauls) and quite lawfully. There was no imposed liturgical book. The Roman church herself was very conservative in liturgical practice: but she made no effort to have her own custom accepted outside her own metropolitan area. Moreover, in the two sacramentaries used at Rome in Gregory's day, (the old Gelasian and the new Gregorian) many Sundays were, in the language of the day, 'vacant': that is, all the variable parts of the mass, scripture readings, psalm verses, collects, etc., were left to the discretion of the celebrant. All the Sundays between Pentecost and Advent were thus 'vacant', and also the Sundays between Epiphany and Lent.

What Augustine had particularly in mind in this query, however, was probably the differences between the Roman rite and the 'Gallican' rite, which was an old rite originating from Milan in the fourth century, at a time when Milan and not Rome was the imperial capital. It had spread in the fifth century from Milan to the Gauls, into Spain, to Ireland, and from the Irish missionaries in Scotland to the Christians in northern Britain. The Gallican rite supplied the variable scripture readings, psalms and collects for the Sundays from Advent to Epiphany and Lent to Pentecost; and moreover, in the Gauls, it had been enriched by the long ceremonies of the Easter vigil, differing somewhat from those used at Rome, and by ceremonies for the veneration of the holy cross. Augustine sought and obtained permission to use such parts of the Gallican rites as he desired.

THIRD: Augustine asked: What should be the punishment if any man stole anything from a church? Gregory answered that

Augustine could judge best from personal knowledge of the thief, how he could best be corrected. 'Some men who have means yet steal', he said, 'and some steal from want; the penalty should be appropriate, heavy fines or stripes. Though the judge should act with strictness, nevertheless he should act with charity, not in anger; charity should rule the judge's mind and dictate the manner of correction. The thief should restore to the church what he has stolen; but the church must not forfeit heavenly gain by seeking increase of earthly possessions.'

Gregory here answers as a moral theologian, and seems to have had no information of Augustine's practical difficulty in protecting the treasure or ornaments of a church according to the laws of the English. Theft or injury was there punished (if the thief or evildoer were caught) according to the gravity of the offence, and the status of the person injured. To steal anything from the king was a very grave offence, but progressively less so from persons in lower grades of society. Now Augustine, and his churches (unlike the king and his hall or the nobleman and his hall, or the freeman and his house) had as yet no recognised status, nor could the pope give him one. Eventually the difficulty was solved when the king in his moot laid down that theft of God's property and the church's should be compensated at a rate twelve fold as heavy as that for theft of a freeman's (see p. 90). This was good protection: for, at the same time, it was laid down that robbery from the king should be compensated nine fold (nine times that paid to a freeman). Bishops, clergy and monks, however, could not fight a robber as well as a freeman in his house or the king's servants in his hall, for they could not bear arms, so that the thief was more likely to make his escape with the goods stolen. However much Augustine's messengers in 601 tried to explain their difficulties to Pope Gregory, he could not well understand the intricacies of Anglo-Saxon law.

FOURTH AND FIFTH: Augustine here asked the difficult question of how he should deal with the question of marriage between near relations, beginning with the question: Could two brothers with the same father and mother marry two sisters who had the same father and mother? Gregory said, Certainly: there was nothing in the scriptures to forbid it. In the Bedan text, Augustine is made to ask in the fifth query: Outside which (numerical) generation ought the faithful to contract marriage with a relation? and is it lawful to marry a stepmother and a kinswoman?

This fifth query and answer certainly do not belong to the days of Augustine and Gregory, when the numbering of generations (first, second, third, etc. generations) was not yet in use. In their days, canon law and indeed Roman law, forbade marriage with the different grades of kinswomen or kinsmen by name. If Gregory had been asked 'within how many generations' [*ad quotam generationem*], which implies a numbering of generations, he would have answered (as the table of kindred and affinity in the Book of Common Prayer), 'a man may not marry his grandmother, his grandfather's wife, his wife's grandmother', and so on down the list of specified relations; though in Latin, most of these relations had a special name. He would say, 'A man may not marry his *noverca* [stepmother], *sobrina*' [first cousin], etc.

Gregory's supposed answer in the Bedan version is thus shown to be unauthentic by reason of the terms in which it is couched; but it is the more impossible because the answer allows the faithful to marry 'within the third and fourth generation'. The history of the reckoning of generations is somewhat complex, and is indeed a double history; Roman law reckoned generations (in the matter of claiming inheritance in the law courts) counting from the claimant up to his common ancestor and down to the person from whom he claimed the property, while the Germanic nations who had settled in Europe counted simply back to the ancestor. Thus by Roman law a nephew claiming to inherit his uncle's property did it as within the third generation, counting from the nephew to his father as one, to his grandfather (the common ancestor) as two, down to the uncle as three. A nephew might not marry his aunt, or a man his niece, in canon law, for they were within the third generation. Yet Pope Gregory, in the Bedan version, said that such a marriage was lawful: which all canonists have found a difficulty ever since. Indeed, within a very few years, the missionary Boniface, when he received a copy of this answer in the manuscript of Bede's *Ecclesiastical History,* could not believe his eyes, and wrote both to Nothelm, archbishop of Canterbury, and to the Roman *scrinium* itself, asking for authentic copies of the

Gregorian answer. The notaries of the *scrinium* replied that no such answer was enrolled; and, indeed, the other form of the tractate, the capitular form, is without this answer.

The explanation of the anomalous answer in the Bedan form is that its author, writing for Germanic people, used the form of counting generations which they used: that is, he counted back simply to the common ancestor of bride and bridegroom, but not, as in Roman law, up to the common ancestor and down the other side. Thus, by the Germanic reckoning, he made Pope Gregory declare that first cousins and the children of first cousins might be allowed to marry, as it were, by concession: 'It is necessary that they should lawfully be allowed to marry.' No notary could have thus written this marriage insertion for, even in Bede's day, he would have used the enumeration of Roman law; but it is possible that Nothelm himself, afterwards archbishop and already, as a priest, with a pastoral outlook, could have made the insertion, using the numeration familiar to Englishmen.

The matter has been explained, not only for its bearing on the difficulties of the missionaries, but because this inserted clause has been the ground on which the authenticity of the whole tractate as Gregorian was long disputed.

The next question in Augustine's series was, for him, of immediate practical importance: granted that he could get Æthelberht's support, political and financial, to provide more bishops, how was he in fact to consecrate them?

SIXTH: If a journey of great length is involved, so that the bishops cannot conveniently assemble, ought a single bishop to ordain a bishop without the presence of other bishops? Gregory answered: 'Since indeed you yourself are the only bishop in the church of the English, you cannot ordain a bishop save in the absence of other bishops. For when are bishops going to come from the Gauls to be present as witnesses to the ordination of a bishop? But we wish your fraternity so to ordain bishops that these bishops shall be separated by no long interval from one another, so that there shall be no such (future) need in the ordination of a bishop (of ordination by a single bishop), but that other shepherds, whose presence is very useful, may and should easily assemble. When therefore by God's help bishops shall be ordained in places adjacent to each other, throughout all these bishoprics no ordination of a bishop shall take place without the presence of three or four bishops.'

Gregory went on to justify this ruling, which actually rested on a canon of the council of Nicaea, by a spiritual analogy. When a wedding is celebrated in the world, guests are invited, to share in the joy of those now married; so in this spiritual ordination, a man is joined to God by this sacred mystery, and others should assemble who shall rejoice in the promotion of the bishop ordained and pray to God for his protection.

The pope clearly disliked sanctioning consecration by a single bishop, as contravening a notable canon, but he regarded consecration by one bishop as valid; indeed, he speaks of other bishops assembled for the consecration as 'witnesses'. It is very doubtful if he was acquainted with the Celtic practice of ordaining bishops for residence in their monasteries or 'llans' by only one bishop; he speaks elsewhere of these (Celtic) bishops as 'bishops'; he knew rather that in the Mediterranean countries some bishops when dying had ordained their own successors, and that this practice had been disapproved. He recommended to Augustine the norm of canonical practice, without questioning the validity of ordination by one bishop in case of necessity. Augustine, in fact, did consecrate Mellitus and Justus alone.

SEVENTH: How ought we to act with regard to the bishops of the Gauls and of the Britains? (the plural because the emperor Severus had divided Britain into two provinces, and the emperor Diocletian into four, to which a fifth was added later: it was as correct to speak of 'the Britains' as 'the Gauls'). Gregory answered:

> We have awarded you no authority over the bishops of the Gauls, for from old times the bishop of Arles has been wont to receive the pallium from my predecessors, and we certainly should not remove an authority once received. [Arles had been the metropolitan city of the whole praetorian prefecture of the Gauls, after Trier had lost this status through the barbarian threat to the Rhine frontier.] But if it should so fall out that your fraternity should cross over into the province of the Gauls, you should take joint action with the bishop of Arles so that if there are any faults among the bishops, they should be corrected. . . . For we have sent him a letter, that when you are present in Gaul he should aid

you with his whole endeavour, and restrain whatever in the manner of life of the bishops is contrary to the command of our creator. You yourself cannot judge the bishops of the Gauls who are beyond your authority; but by persuasion and gentle words and showing them the example of a good life do you recall the minds of bad men to the study of sanctity. . . . Put not the sickle of judgment into the harvest committed to another man. . . . But whatever needs to be done with authority, let it be done in co-operation with the aforesaid bishop of Arles. . . .

But all the bishops of the Britains we commit to your fraternity, that the untaught may be taught, the weak strengthened by persuasion and the perverse corrected by authority.

Gregory thus made clear to Augustine that he could not intervene to reform, on his own sole authority, those evils of simony and irregular life that Gregory believed to exist in the Gauls, and of which he had himself written to Queen Brunhild and the bishop of Arles. His hope that Augustine himself might yet be travelling through Gaul was not fulfilled. As to the bishops of 'the Britains', the Celtic bishops: his knowledge of them must have depended on the information afforded by Augustine's messengers, and possibly he had heard rumours of the Celtic monk, Columbanus, who was working in the Vosges and among the Alemanni from 590 onwards. But Columbanus only reached northern Italy some years after Gregory's death, dying there in 615. There is no evidence that Pope Gregory had received Celtic pilgrims in Rome, for the history of pilgrimage in these early centuries is obscure. It would seem then that Augustine's messengers had communicated to him all that was known of the Celtic Christians in Canterbury; they had bishops, but they must be 'uninstructed', for they did not seem to rule churches, for instance, but to reside in monasteries under an abbot. Since the Angles and Saxons were still conquering the Britons westward and north-ward by occasional fighting, Augustine's knowledge of them and their bishops was limited.

In the EIGHTH question Augustine asked whether a pregnant woman might be baptised, and sundry other questions about conditions which might entail what could be called liturgical defilement: ought the person in such cases to approach the altar or even enter a church? Gregory answered as a moral theologian and in some detail, stressing the need to baptise a woman who seemed likely to die in childbirth, and the need to allow a baptised woman to receive holy communion in the days after childbirth, if she so desired.

The NINTH answer also deals at length with the question whether a man may receive communion or celebrate the mass after the illusions of the night. The long answer quotes a dictum of Pope Gregory in his homilies on the Sunday Gospels; he said, about temptation, that every sin is fulfilled in three manners, namely, by suggestion, by pleasure in the suggestion and by consent. It is likely that this long answer, which amounts to a homily, was the work of one who had studied Pope Gregory's homilies, rather than of Gregory himself: he did not usually quote his own earlier works verbally.

Some collections of papal letters have also a TENTH question about the relics of 'the martyr Sixtus': for this, see Chapter 5.

It may fairly be assumed that the questions and answers sent to Bede do indicate the matters which Augustine held important, matters on which, in his missionary see, he sought for papal guidance and authorisations. They are very far from illuminating the day to day conduct of his mission, the day to day contact with the king, his court and the young princes, the instruction of candidates for baptism, the actual baptisms after the long vigils of the eves of Christmas, Easter and Pentecost, the feeding of the poor in the long starvation of the winter months and the healing of the sick brought to him. There was the day to day business of building small stone churches at Canterbury and Rochester, and arranging for the support of Mellitus in London. There was the fatherly care for his own clergy and monks, for no community flourishes without the day to day care of its bishop or abbot. There was the ceaseless hostility of some of Æthelberht's subjects, the priests of the old sanctuaries and the nobles and thegns who supported them. The king constrained no man to become a Christian, and, indeed, it is unlikely that he could have done so; after his death pagan discontent nearly overthrew the church. About all the details of the missionaries' daily life, Bede says very little.

A Celtic scribe, writing down what he knew of a saint's life and miracles, would have had many stories of the saint's gentleness and holiness in his day to day contacts with the simple, the sick and the poor; to him it was clear that even the animals, being God's creation, realised the holiness and compassion of God's servant. The sea creatures sat on Columba's feet to warm them, and the old horse came to bid him farewell when he was dying. For Brendan on his boat, with Easter at hand and no land in sight, a great whale raised its shoulders high above the surface of the waves, so that it formed dry land; Brendan and his company celebrated Easter upon it, being there one day and two nights. And when they had entered into their boats, the whale dived into the sea at once. And this was fitting, for the Celtic scribe knew that the scriptures said that Jonah was in the whale's belly three days and three nights and the whale cast him up alive, and he became a symbol of Christ's resurrection. To the Celtic scribe, Brendan and Jonah and the whale all being in the mind of God, the whale well knew that Easter must be celebrated, and that Brendan and his company had no land at hand, so he knew that he must rear up his back and provide an island. To the Celtic mind, this was a miracle, but not in any way an unlikely miracle. To the Celts, with only the Iron Age behind them and the Christian sun newly risen upon them, the mercy of God was very plainly visible; the brightness of his majesty spangled in their eyes.

But Augustine came from another world. Behind him was the old, learned civilisation of the Mediterranean, a world full of books and law and the records of imperial government. Gregory who sent him, and Bede who recorded his labours, both belonged to this Latin world. Both of them believed in miracles, and Bede attested that God granted miracles at Augustine's prayer, and Pope Gregory warned him not to fall into the sin of pride at such heavenly graciousness: but these signs were not the kindly, domestic miracles that shone across the humble and poor lives of the Celtic saints. The little cat caught no fish for Augustine; and, if she had, the grave fathers at Canterbury would not have passed on such a story to Bede.

Augustine's work, like that of the Celtic clergy, was apostolic. He was planting the Christian Church in a barbarous island, and he was planning its structure as he knew it in his world. The newly baptised Anglo-Saxons should be part of Christ's Church and share with the men of Gaul and the men of Italy

and the men of Greece the apostolic faith, and the Christian
scriptures which recorded God's intention that all men should
be saved. They must have bishops who were the apostolic
teachers and guaranteed the rightness, the orthodoxy, of the
faith taught. Since there must be bishops Augustine felt he
must set about establishing bishops' sees, with clergy to help
the bishops teach the faith to the heathen.

The establishment of such sees depended on Æthelberht's
power to build churches for the new bishops and provide
endowment for their *familiae* of clergy. Augustine consecrated
two bishops, for Durobrevis and Londinium. If Durovernum
on the Stour had been the natural road centre for east Kent in
Roman times, Durobrevis on the Medway, which flowed
through the great gap in the north downs northwards to the
Thames mouth, was the natural road and river centre for west
Kent. The Watling Street from Durovernum crossed the Medway just to the north of Durobrevis, branching into lesser roads
to the Thames shore while making its way to Londinium; the
Medway itself brought traffic from the Vale of Kent up to
Durobrevis and the Watling Street. We do not know the chieftains who ruled the Kentish tribes under Æthelberht, though
we have hints that there may have been one or two sub-kings.
In his own kingdom, however, Æthelberht had power and land
enough to build a church dedicated to St Andrew, and for this
new see Augustine consecrated Justus as bishop. The king gave
'territories and possessions' sufficient to support the new bishop
and his familia.

The same year Augustine consecrated the abbot from the
Gauls, Mellitus, to be bishop of Londinium. Here Æthelberht
built a church dedicated to St Paul, up on the high ground
north of the Thames where the old Roman Forum had stood;
the road from the Roman bridge across the Thames ran up into
the Forum. There had been a Roman bishop at Londinium as
early as the council of Arles in 314; where he had his church we
do not know, but Æthelberht and Augustine set the new church
well within the old Roman city, with Saeberht's acquiescence.
Again, it was Æthelberht who built the church and provided
the lands.

Both the churches at Durobrevis and Londinium were so
much built over in the course of centuries that no trace of their

walls or foundations have been discovered by the archaeologists. But it seems that they must have been similar to Augustine's monastery church of SS Peter and Paul, and one or two other Kentish churches slightly later in date. They were of stone, and built by foreign workmen, probably Italians, skilled in the use of Roman brick. The rectangular nave would have ended in a semi-circular apse, perhaps separated from the nave by a triple arcade. A low stone altar, probably a cube in shape, would have stood on the chord of the apse, and around this apse ran a stone seat for the clergy, with a seat slightly raised for the bishop, in the centre, behind the altar. Usually, however, the bishop himself would have celebrated the mysteries, standing by seventh-century custom before the altar. In earlier days he had stood behind it. Chambers or *porticus*, for the offerings or the vesting of the clergy, would, according to custom, have been built to right and left of the altar, and all, in Augustine's day, on the same level; the building of crypts or 'confessions' for the martyrs' relics, with a raised 'chancel' above, were not yet. Such relics as Pope Gregory had sent Augustine from Rome in 601 (and relics there must have been to accompany the dedications to St Andrew and St Paul) would have been enclosed within the altars.

## CHAPTER 5

# Augustine and the 'Bishops of Britain'

POPE GREGORY had committed 'all the bishops of Britain' to
Augustine's care. He knew very little about them, less than
about the Syrian and Armenian bishops who at times appeared
in Rome and stayed in the monasteries of the Greeks. He did
not doubt that there were bishops over all the world, for had not
the apostles preached to the limits of the known world? In the
office of the Common of an Apostle the chapter ran: 'Ye are not
strangers and pilgrims but fellow citizens of the saints and the
domestics of God: ye are built upon the foundation of the
apostles and prophets.' To which the choir sang in response,
and many times a year he sang it with them: 'Their sound is
gone out to all the world and their words to the ends of the
earth.' Certainly the preaching of the apostles, so long ago, had
reached the ends of the earth. Where they had preached, there
would be bishops. But about the bishops of Ireland and the
Britains in his own day he knew only by vague rumour and the
little that Augustine's messengers could tell him.

The studies of Celticists and archaeologists have given us
much more knowledge of the state of Christianity in 'the
Britains' than that possessed by Augustine or Gregory. We
know a very little about the Christianity of Roman times which
had survived even in the part of Britain conquered by the
Anglo-Saxons, and much more about the British Christianity
which had been driven back to the west in the hundred and
fifty years between the first Saxon settlements and Augustine's
coming. We know that the Irish Channel was a kind of Christian
Mediterranean, running between the Christians of the British
and Scottish coasts, and those of Ireland; and that this Celtic
Christianity was very old. Its roots went back to Roman
Britain on the British side of the Channel, and northern
Britain and western Gaul on the other; it was a Christianity
that had survived in a tribal society in the one case, and had

been preached in a tribal society in the other. Irish and British saints and pilgrims passed freely across the Irish Channel, which was indeed 'their sea': but since the advent of the pagan English, their only other contacts had been with Gaul. It was a Christian civilisation that had survived in isolation, and to travellers from the Mediterranean it must have seemed a hundred and fifty years behind the times: if, indeed, such travellers were able to ascribe differences of ecclesiastical practice to historical causes.

As to the little that we know, and that Augustine probably did not know, about surviving remnants of Christianity in Britain: Bede says that Augustine was given leave 'to repair churches', but these would mainly have been ruined buildings, with no congregations. The house church at Lullingstone, which had consisted of four rooms in a Roman villa set aside for Christian worship and perhaps the dwelling of a priest, was much used in the reign of Constantine II (337–40) and survived later, but how much later there is no evidence. No one knows, either, how long the basilica of Silchester was used for Christian worship, or the rooms of other house churches in villas. At some point, the owners of these villas, and the bishops in the cities of Roman Britain, fled to the west, or to Brittany.

It is of interest, however, that the little evidence of survival that we have includes that about the great 'martyrium' of England, the tomb of Alban, the first martyr. In the fourth, fifth and sixth centuries, in Africa, in Italy and throughout the Christian world men went to pray by the graves or the tombs where the martyrs slept, especially on the anniversary of their 'birthday' into heaven; and where so much prayer was poured, miracles of healing were vouchsafed. Gildas in his *De Excidio* recounts the martyrdoms of Alban and of the Welsh martyrs, Aaron and Julius, and he adds that there were many more martyrs in Britain, and many 'martyria' erected when the persecutions ceased; these were again destroyed or left deserted when the pagan Saxons invaded the country. Bede recounted Alban's martyrdom, using Gildas, but he added that 'a church of wonderful workmanship worthy of his martyrdom was built near by, and many cures were wrought there up till this day'. When King Offa, later, wished to build a minster in Alban's honour, he knew well where to build it. It was, indeed, not

unlikely that if Christianity survived under the pagan conquerors at all, it would be where prayers were offered at the
martyria and miracles of healing followed. Such prayers and
miracles imply some sort of a surviving local Christian
congregation.

Against the background of this meagre evidence about the
martyria, one letter found in some manuscripts as part of the
tractate of Gregory's answers to Augustine may possibly refer
to a martyrium at Canterbury.[1] This letter was not sent up by
Hadrian to Bede for inclusion in his *Ecclesiastical History* and
does not appear in that work. It is found in some of the canonical
collections of Gregory's letters, and in one notably early manuscript of the capitular text now at Copenhagen. It appears
there without the names of inquirer or respondent, and in no
manuscript otherwise than among these answers of Gregory to
Augustine; it is usually headed 'Obsecratio Augustini' (the
Supplication of Augustine) and is, in fact, a request for the true
relics of 'the martyr Sixtus'. It is in bad Latin, and would
appear to have been transcribed, in summary form, from a
defective papyrus original, or to have been badly transcribed.
The request and answer run:

> In the tenth chapter you have asked that relics of Saint Sixtus
> the martyr should be sent by us. We have done what you asked;
> so that the people who in a certain place are said to venerate the
> body of Saint Sixtus the martyr (about which your fraternity has
> grave doubts whether he was a saint), shall receive the gracious
> gifts [*beneficia*] of a most holy and certain martyr, and not venerate
> an uncertain one. It seems to me that if a body which is popularly
> believed to be that of a martyr does not shine with miracles, nor do
> any old people exist who attest that they have heard from their
> parents the order of his passion, that then the relics you have
> asked for should be set somewhere apart and the place where the
> aforesaid body lies shall be shut off, neither shall the people be
> allowed to desert the certain relics and venerate the uncertain.

The original petitions may, indeed, have referred to some
nameless martyr, for there is no known Sixtus cult in Canter-

---

[1] For this answer about the relics of the martyr Sixtus, see Deanesly and
Grosjean, *art. cit.* 28–32. Since the writing of that article, the present writer's
assessment of the survival of the cult of the martyrs at their place of burial has
led her to accept as probable the survival of a local cult of a martyr Sixtus in
Britain, and most probably at Canterbury.

bury, at Kent possibly; possibly the answer was not even Gregorian. Nevertheless, the query is not found associated with any other pope's letters, or by itself: it is found only in association with the answers of Gregory to Augustine. Though it was not used by Bede, it may fairly be allowed that letters dealing with the veneration of uncertain relics were private to the archbishop recipient, and not intended for the wide publicity which insertion in Bede's history would give them. If the reply is genuinely Gregorian, it could only have referred to relics under Augustine's jurisdiction, which did not extend beyond Kent.

The 'most certain relics of the martyr Sixtus' which the pope promised to send would have been pallia laid against the tomb of Pope Sixtus II, who was martyred, along with his deacon Lawrence and their companions, in the Valerianic persecution of 258. The veneration of Pope Sixtus at first and in Gregory's day exceeded that of his companion martyrs; later, reverence for St Lawrence eclipsed it. It is possible that Sixtus, as the name of a famous martyr, was taken as a name by some candidate for the clerical or monastic order after 258; the name occurs in episcopal lists between 258 and the persecutions under Diocletian. It is not impossible that a British Sixtus should have been martyred in the Diocletianic persecution at the beginning of the fourth century. If so, it is likely that he perished in a city, for the Roman government of Britain does not appear to have pursued fugitive Christians into the countryside. Alban was brought to trial in Verulam, Aaron and Julius in Caerleon. Durovernum was the Roman capital of Kent, and if there were a Kentish martyrium among the many that Gildas asserted existed, it would probably be at Durovernum, or in one of the cemeteries just outside. Professor Jocelyn Toynbee has pointed out that the site of 'St Martins', outside the walls of Durovernum, is possibly that of a martyrium; it lies the same distance from the city walls as does the martyrium of St Severin, the patron saint of Trier. It could be that Augustine found the people venerating 'the martyr Sixtus' in Liuthard's church, for this was actually chosen as the place where Queen Bertha should worship, presumably as the most obvious holy site at Canterbury where Christian worship might best be renewed; but this is speculation.

In any case, if it was indeed Augustine who found the people venerating a nameless martyr who did not coruscate with miracles, and about whose passion no old man could tell him the course as heard from his parents: about whom he knew no more than that there was a tomb which the people venerated, perhaps with the name Sixtus carved upon it—if this was so, then perhaps access to the tomb was blocked, and another altar elsewhere dedicated with the relics of the true Sixtus laid up within it. But reverence for such pallia was very different from that popularly and spontaneously given to a martyr's tomb by those who lived near and by pilgrims. It would not be expected to attract more reverence than the other numerous relics sent by Pope Gregory, who was in the habit of sending many relics to bishops he wished to honour. Sixtus does not occur as a proper name thereafter in Britain, but pre-conquest bishops kept their Anglo-Saxon names. Relics of St Pancras must have been sent for the dedication of the church of St Pancras in the grounds of Augustine's abbey, but Pancras does not occur among the names of English ecclesiastics, regular or secular: nor does Lawrence. If a British martyr Sixtus slept at Canterbury, Augustine's doubts suppressed the cult, nor did the relics of the pope and martyr Sixtus inspire any reverence noted in records or archaeology or name-taking.

Of the Celtic bishops in Britain of whom Gregory and Augustine knew so little, we know something. We know that in the Celtic churches organisation was tribal and monastic, for the sub-Roman cities had decayed before and after the Romans went and were no longer large population groups: they could not, as in Gaul, be the centre of a territorial episcopate. The Christian clergy had become monastic, living under an abbot in a small monastery or 'llan', a holy spot: the word 'llan' has the same root as 'sanctus'. The larger llans usually had regional names like Llandaff (the llan on the Tavy); the smaller, outlying llans were often called by their holy founder's name, Llansannam in Denbighshire, Llantwit (for Llan Illtud). The monks of these llans, or their abbots, travelled about their own regions, to preach, baptise and, at times, heal their people; all the monks were clergy and there were no other clergy. The greatest of the holy founders, David, Cyngar, Gildas and the rest, were the sons of kings or tribal chiefs, and the livelihood of their monks was provided by their own title to land; but a holy monk without land might be provided for by some king whom he pleased. The Celtic language of Britain may be called Welsh; though it differed in the different regions, all the regional tongues were derived from the same parent language. The Anglo-Saxons called the Britons 'Welsh', and the Welsh of Cornwall and Somerset would, at the time, have spoken a tongue understandable to the Welsh of Wales or Cumberland, though less so to the Gaels and Picts north of Hadrian's Wall. Old Irish had come from the same parent stock, but had suffered some sound changes when the tribes who spoke it had long ago settled in Ireland. But it must have been understood to some extent by the Welsh, for there was much coming and going across the Irish Channel, and the holy and learned abbot Gildas was requested by an Irish king to come and advise about the liturgy of the mass.

In short, though there was certainly no one central church government among the Celtic Christians, no great general synods to which the abbots and bishops of all the countries bordering the Irish Channel were summoned, yet there was a similarity of custom, a consciousness of having received the faith very long ago, that gave the Celts confidence and even pride. Their monk-clergy read Cassian and the lives of the desert Fathers and practised an asceticism nourished on their writings as well as the scriptures. The Celts had confidence in their present and their past.

The Anglo-Saxons of Britain they regarded as their pagan enemies, who had taken most of their country from them, and who still sought to push their frontier farther to the west and north by force of arms. This fluctuating frontier ran from the Channel northwards through Somerset, past the Archenfield of Herefordshire, up the present Welsh border, and through Cumberland. The British in Northumbria were still fighting hard against the northern Angles in 597; it was only fifty years earlier, in 547, that Ida, the first king of the northern Angles, made settlements at Tynemouth and along the coast; in his son's time the Angles were still struggling to maintain their foothold. They were besieged for three days and nights in Holy Island. The pagan king Æthelfrith (592–616) was the first

Northumbrian king to extend his conquests inland and establish a real Northumbrian kingdom. The northern Britons still fought back.

The Celtic Christians were then little inclined to receive any overtures from Augustine without suspicion. They were the Christian people of Britain and always had been: they had fought for their faith and their way of life against the pagan. They were still fighting the pagan, though now, 150 years after the Anglo-Saxon coming, they seemed to have held him back to a fairly stationary line. Inevitably, any advance to them made by a bishop under Anglo-Saxon protection appeared an effort to extend Anglo-Saxon influence over them.

Augustine must have known very little about the local Celtic churches with whose leaders he wished to get in touch in order to carry out Pope Gregory's instructions. We know little ourselves. In the south-west, St Cyngar had been the patron saint of Somerset, travelling from north Wiltshire through north Somerset in pastoral preaching journeys; one of the stories his people told about him was that he stuck his staff into the ground, to make the place holy for a preaching or baptism, and it turned into a yew tree. Afterwards, there was a little church there. His llans were at Llancyngar (Congresbury) and Banwell; he was preaching from about 530 onwards, and in his life-time the conquering Anglo-Saxons possessed themselves of Salisbury (552). The very holy llan at Yniswitrin lay westward, where the river Parret ran into the Bristol Channel; it was still in Welsh country in Augustine's time, and the English king Cenwalh did not fight his way there till 658. Farther west still, the monastery at Bodmin cherished the memory of St Petroc. It was the bishops, teachers and abbots of the south-west region who would seem to have had easiest access to the meeting place near the Bristol Channel that Bede says was called 'Augustine's Oak' in his day.

The abbots and bishops from Wales were also accessible, for there was a trade route from south Wales across the Bristol Channel, and monks from the region of Caerleon and Llandaff might travel round the river mouth of the Severn, or cross the river in boats. The monastery of Dewi (David) at St David's was a great house. Dewi had died only in or about the year 588. Gildas, the great abbot, had died, according to the Anglo-Saxon Chronicle, only in 570, and Samson, his contemporary, had

lived first in a monastery on Caldy Island, then in one on the
Severn, before leaving Britain for Brittany. All the most famous
Welsh monk saints, Dewi, Gildas, Teilo, Cadoc, Padarn, Daniel
and Samson had lived and flourished in the middle of the sixth
century, and Augustine would have had to deal with the generation of monks that succeeded them. Of many of them their
'Lives', written later, recounted that they went on pilgrimage,
some even to Jerusalem and Rome; and though these stories can
be ascribed to the writers' confusion with what might have happened in a later age projected back into the saint's life as well
befitting him, there is no suggestion at all of any hostility to the
churches of Gaul or the see of Peter. Rome was very distant and
very holy; Peter slept there; men naturally desired to pray at
his tomb, just as the empress Helena had desired to discover the
place Golgotha and the holy cross. The monks of Llantwit or
the Bangor of St Deiniol would have welcomed a monk from
Egypt or Lérins or Tours or the monastery *ad clivum Scauri*;
but a bishop of the Anglo-Saxons, sent under the protection of
the *bretwalda* and the conquering king of the West Saxons—
that was another matter.

Bede recounts Augustine's efforts to get into touch with the
Welsh 'bishops and teachers' and persuade them to accept his
primatial authority and join him in his efforts to convert the
English. He was really expecting the Christians of one civilisation, to which their church order was fitted, to accept him as
archbishop in the continental sense, in a hierarchy fitted originally to the cities of the empire in the west. There was no primatial authority in their own churches; the abbot bishop of St
David's, for instance, claimed no authority over the great
Bangor in Flintshire. It was to be expected that the Celts would
refuse to fall in with his suggestion.

After recounting all that he knew of Augustine's work to
build the little church of the Saviour at Canterbury and that of
his new monastery, and digressing to speak of the life and death
of Pope Gregory, Bede goes on to speak of Augustine's efforts
to establish relations with the British bishops.

In the meanwhile, Augustine, using the help of King
Æthelberht, summoned to a conference the bishops and doctors
of the nearest province of the Britons, in the place which up till
today is called in the tongue of the English, 'Augustine's Oak',

that is (in Latin) 'robur Augustini'; and he began to persuade them with brotherly admonition that they would maintain the catholic peace with him and undertake the labour of preaching the gospel to the gentiles for the Lord's sake, in common with him.

Here Bede, having reported what appears to be the Canterbury tradition of Augustine's opening, goes on to speak of what he took to be the chief difference between the church observances of the two parties: the Celts had a different computus for deciding the date of Easter. 'Maintaining the catholic peace' would seem, however, to refer more naturally to ending the enmity between Britons and Anglo-Saxons, which must have been a great obstacle to any joint effort at evangelism. Though it was, of course, out of place and impracticable to discuss political difficulties at a church synod, which would limit the discussion to properly ecclesiastical subjects and differences, it has been suggested by modern historians that controversy about the dating of Easter had not yet become acute in western Europe. Apart from Bede's, possibly antedated, assertion that the matter was raised at this meeting, the struggle would seem to have begun when Columbanus in Gaul wrote questioning the holy see in this matter. He seems to have regarded the difficulty as a mathematical one, about which he could argue on equal terms with the pope. When the great subject of formal acceptance of the authority of the Petrine see by the Celtic churches was discussed at Whitby in 664, the dating of Easter was clearly a matter to be settled, as involving an open and inconvenient difference of practice between the Celtic and the Rome-taught Christians, and such discussion fits into the general history of the Paschal controversy; it is less certain that Bede was right in alleging it as the chief difficulty between Augustine and those whom he met at 'Augustine's Oak'. There could have been no practical difficulty in celebrating Easter at different times in Llantwit and Canterbury: a wide barrier of unconverted pagans intervened. Be that as it may, Bede continues:

For they (the Celts) did not observe Easter Sunday at the right date, but as falling between the twenty-fourth and the twentieth day of the moon, this computation falling within a cycle of eighty-four years. And they did many other things contrary to ecclesiastical unity. And when a long discussion had been held and they would

not give assent to the prayers or the exhortations or the reproofs
of Augustine and his companions, but preferred to follow their
own traditions rather than the universal ones which the whole
Christian world agree in holding, Augustine, the holy father,
brought this long and wearisome struggle to an end and said: 'We
implore God, who maketh men to dwell together in the house of
the Father, that he would teach us by heavenly signs which tradition should be followed and by what ways we should hasten to
enter into his heavenly kingdom.'

Then he goes on to relate how a blind man was brought into
the conference, and when the Celtic bishops (*sacerdotibus*) had
tried and could not cure him, Augustine knelt and prayed and
the blind man received his sight. All men acclaimed Augustine
as the herald of the light divine. The Britons admitted that the
way Augustine had preached to them was indeed the way of
righteousness, but they said they could not without the leave of
their seniors abandon their ancient customs. They asked, therefore, that a second synod should be held which many should
attend.

This seeking of a sign from God on a matter which human
intelligence could not decide would have seemed both to
Augustine's followers and the Britons perhaps daring, but not
unprecedented either in the scriptures or in the life of the church.
Had not God sent fire upon Elijah's altar, consuming the burnt
sacrifice, when all the prophets of Baal crying aloud and cutting
themselves with knives could get no such fiery answer from
their gods? Did not all men know that St Helena, seeing the
true cross and finding the three crosses that had stood on Golgotha, had bidden the three crosses to be laid in turn beside a
sick woman: and God had, by healing the woman when the
third cross was laid beside her, showed which was indeed the
cross that had borne the Lord of glory? To Hadrian and Bede
the miracle shown on the blind man was entirely fitting and
consonant with the purpose of God. Bede continues:

And when this was decided, there came, as they [the men of
Canterbury] tell, seven bishops of the Britons and many most
learned men, and chiefly from the most noble monastery of them
all, which is called in the tongue of the English, Bancornabyrig
[Bangor in Flintshire], of which Dinoot [Donatus] is said at the

time to have been abbot. And when they were going to the afore-said council, they went to take advice of a holy and prudent man who was living the life of an anchorite among them. They asked him whether they ought to abandon their own tradition at the preaching of Augustine? And he replied: 'If he is a man of God, follow him.' And they said: 'And how shall we prove whether he is or not?' And he said: 'the Lord said, Take my yoke upon you and learn of me, for I am meek and lowly of heart. If therefore Augustine is meek and lowly of heart, give heed to him, for he beareth the yoke of Christ himself and invites you to bear it with him; but if he is not meek, but proud, it is clear that he is not of God, nor should you give heed to his word.' And when they said again: 'And how shall we discern this?', he said: 'Make sure that he and his people come first to the place of the synod, and if he rise when you approach, do you, knowing he is the servant of Christ, hear him with meekness; if however he scorn you and will not rise to go to meet you, you who are greater in numbers than he is, let him in turn be scorned by you.'

They did as he said. And thus it was done: and when they were approaching, Augustine sat on in his chair. And they seeing this were at once angered and strove to contradict all that he said.

This is a famous account of a famous interview, about which some points should be noted. The place of the second synod is not given, but since Bede stresses the presence of learned men from the great Bangor (an Irish word meaning community) of north Wales, the meeting would presumably have taken place much farther to the north than that at 'Augustine's Oak'. Augustine may have followed the old Watling Street, running diagonally across England, from Dover to Canterbury, Canterbury to London and London to Chester. It is likely that the old street, laid out by the Roman army surveyor, would still have survived in good enough condition to enable travellers to take a fairly straight course from Londinium to north Wales.

It is notable also that the abbot of Bangor did not attend the synod. Like the abbot of most great Celtic monasteries, he must have had certain claustral bishops for those rites of ordination and consecration which only a bishop may perform. It has indeed been suggested that the seven bishops who attended the synod were the bishops who headed the seven septs of the great monastery of Bangor, under the abbot. Whether this is the case or not, the seven bishops who attended must have been claustral bishops or abbot bishops, for there were as yet in Wales no territorial bishops. The status which Augustine attributed to bishops, when in fact most abbots were kings' sons, or sons of princes, men who had attained their position many years before custom allowed their consecration as bishops, and when their bishops were holy and reverend senior monks with no decisive power as against that of the abbot, this status must have been a difficulty in a synod of this kind. It is not difficult to infer from the abbot's absence that he had no great enthusiasm for this meetnig with Augustine.

As to the anchorite's advice, it was indeed prudent from the Celtic point of view. Bede's word 'sella' implies a chair, such as the magistrate used in court, the rhetor when he lectured to his standing audience, and the bishop when he taught from his chair. 'All the bishops of Britain,' Pope Gregory had said, 'we commit to your care.' To rise to meet them would have been to admit equality, to abandon the commission to teach. Augustine sat on in his chair, and the bishops and doctors reflected on the words of the gospel so appropriately suggested to them by the anchorite. An old civilisation shrank away from one which was more modern.

Augustine spoke of his willingness to accept with equanimity many things in their custom different from 'ours: even though such customs differ from those of the universal church', provided the Celts would agree to accept the Roman usage in three points: that they should celebrate Easter at its due time, fulfil the ministry of baptism by which we are reborn in God according to the manner of the holy, Roman and apostolic church; and preach the word of God 'with us' to the people of the English. All the other things which the Britons did, though contrary to our custom, 'we will acquiesce in with equanimity'.

This list of points on which uniformity between Celtic and Roman practice Augustine considered essential might have included the dating of Easter, though the struggle about it rose to greater proportions later and the Celts did not give up their reckoning till many years after the later synod of Whitby. The difficulty hinged upon the determination of the March equinox. The great canonist, Dionysius Exiguus, had laid down in 526, in answer to a request for information by the papal *scrinium*, a rule for calculating the date of Easter. 'Easter is the Sunday which follows the fourteenth day of the moon which attains this age on 21 March or immediately after.' This rule he attributed, mistakenly, to the council of Nicaea of 325. The ruling left the equinox, 21 March, to be determined by the secular mathematicians, though Dionysius himself followed the reckoning, or cycle, of the doctors of Alexandria. The Roman church herself, having asked, did not hold herself bound in all cases to follow the ruling, even though she accepted it in general as from the council of Nicaea. Nor did she seek to impose any general ruling on other churches. In the case of Britain, however, a difference of custom on this point came to be held as the major sign that the Celts held to their own tradition as older and equally apostolic; in fact, it emphasised political separation.

Bede next recounts that Augustine foretold to the Celts that if they would not accept peace with their brethren, they must accept war with their enemies: if they would not preach the way of life to the English, they should receive at their hands the judgment of death. Which prophecy, he says, was fulfilled when the mighty heathen king, Æthelfrith of Northumbria, made a very great slaughter of the Britons at the battle of Chester (616). A coalition of British princes had summoned the monks from this same Bangor, Bangor Iscoed, to pray for them as they fought the battle. They were unarmed, but Æthelfrith feared they were magicians who would do him harm and he had some 1,200 of the unarmed monks massacred by his warriors. Bede's implication that this was a punishment for their refusal to accept Augustine's terms is prejudiced and unlike him; usually he writes with sympathy and admiration of the Celtic saints.

Augustine did not succeed, then, in bringing the Celtic churches under his care: that was left for the learned and saintly Archbishop Theodore, who, curiously enough, was sent by the Roman church and the pope's selection, like Augustine himself. But a lot of water had run under the bridge when Archbishop Theodore arrived in Canterbury in 668; and Theodore himself had had a wider experience than Augustine.

## CHAPTER 6

# What Augustine Brought to Britain

THE years Augustine spent in Canterbury were few: he was consecrated bishop in 597 and he died on 26 May, as it is reckoned, in 604. Bede does not give the year: the messengers from Canterbury would know the day of the archbishop's obit, for that would be written into a liturgical calendar, that the anniversary of his death might be duly celebrated with prayers; dating by the year of the incarnation was not, however, in use at the time of Augustine's death, and all that Bede could record with certainty was that this death was in the days of Æthelberht the king. A seven years' episcopate, or even one slightly longer, was in any case short; but the impact of those years on the English nation was very great. It could be said of this *praepositus* from the monastery *ad clivum Scauri,* using the modern idiom, that he had 'started something'. He had brought to the English Latin Christianity and Latin civilisation, or its beginnings. He had brought them at very great risk, and he had worked very hard.

Summarising the impact of Augustine's work on his own and future generations, it may be said that his teaching replaced the Anglo-Saxons' Germanic paganism, their veneration of Thor the thunder god and war god, and Woden the All-Father, with the worship of Christ the Saviour and Redeemer, and 'God the Creator, all-holy, the Lord everlasting, the king of mankind, who created for mortals the world in its beauty, and hung the bright heaven above the children of men'. The impact affected English society through its laws, now for the first time written down, and by bringing a written learning to Kent; by the introduction of stone for building, and of a new style of architecture; by the introduction of the *vita monachica,* with all its developments in the English minsters; and by the use of the Latin liturgy, scriptures and sacramentaries. In short, the impact brought with Latin Christianity much of the Latin civilisation in which it had been set, as Augustine knew it, in Italy.

The laws of the men of Kent at Augustine's coming were folk laws, like those of the other Germanic nations, the Franks, the Lombards or the Visigoths. They were handed down in the memory of freemen and elders in the folk moot, or the king's witan or council of wise men; they consisted of long and detailed tariffs of compensation for injuries. The worst injury to a man was to deprive him of life, and for this the family of the murderer paid a heavy money fine to the family of the murdered man, even if the killing were not premeditated, but the result of a fight or a tavern brawl. This method of atonement for injury was then modern and progressive, for the earlier Germanic method of discouraging homicide was for the murdered man's kin to fight the family of the murderer: the method of the blood feud. A principle in determining the 'wer', worth, of the man killed and for whom money compensation must be paid was that each social class had its known 'wer', and that more must be paid for killing a man of high rank than for killing a freeman, and much more than for killing a slave. The killer would normally be in the same social class as the man killed, and his family be able to pay proportionately. The heaviest penalties of all must be paid for killing a king's servant, nobleman or freeman. All society was graded according to their wergeld: king, nobleman or 'eorl', freeman ('ceorl'), slave ('theow'), and a conquered Briton, called a 'læt', according to the class he was reckoned to be in. Thus a ceorl's wer was, in Kent in Æthelberht's time, 100 shillings, whilst a Briton's might be 80, 60 or 40 shillings, according to his class; but in all cases, less than the free, English ceorl's.[1]

The laws had, moreover, many detailed payments for injuries less than killing: 3 shillings for laying bare a bone, 4 shillings for damage to a bone, 10 or even 20 shillings for damage to the skull, 25 shillings for destroying the hearing of either ear, 50 shillings for knocking out an eye. For each of the front teeth, 4 shillings, and separate payment for destroying each of the fingers, the toes, the nails, and injuring the different parts of the body. It must be remembered that where medicine was so primitive (the man who had to receive medical treatment got 30 shillings compensation), injury to any part of an Anglo-Saxon man's body meant destroying his ability to fight or to work.

[1] See F. L. Attenborough, *Laws*, p. 4

A few other offences besides inflicting bodily injury are specified in the laws: breaking into his house or property, his 'mund', where again the money penalty varies according to the rank of the person whose mund (his private jurisdiction or peace) is infringed; 'the king's mund byrd (or mund breach) shall be 50 shillings'. If a small band of men break into another man's premises, he who breaks in first shall pay 6 shillings, he who comes next 3 shillings, and afterwards each shall pay 1 shilling. There are appropriate penalties for lying with a maiden belonging to the king (less for a grinding slave), for breaking the fence round another man's enclosure, for violating the munds of widows of different social classes, for a man's taking a widow who does not rightly belong to him, for buying a maiden dishonestly (in which case she shall be taken back to her own home and the money returned to him), for robbing a slave on a highway. For all offences less than homicide, men paid a 'bot'. Homicide was 'bootless': 'If one man slays another he shall pay 20 shillings before the grave is closed, and the whole of the wergeld within 40 days.'

All these laws and penalties must have seemed to Augustine very unsafe, because unwritten, used as he was to dealing with notaries and written laws. He must have sat at the folk moot at times, when the king addressed his people, though strictly it was the free men and nobles who declared what the penalty for the offence was. It is not known where Æthelberht addressed his eorls and ceorls, and his bishop with his attendant clergy. At Yeavering, in the far north, recent excavation has shown that King Edwin, Æthelberht's son-in-law and king of Northumbria, had a kind of stadium, a segment of an amphitheatre, built, of course, of timber. The eorls and ceorls of the court, and those who travelled there at his summons, sat or stood on the tiers of rising benches, and heard the king, standing before them, address them: all moots were held in the open air, and such a device enabled the king to be well heard. Durovernum has been too much built over for the post holes of wooden buildings to be discovered by digging; but there was, at any rate, a Roman amphitheatre surviving within the town, and Æthelberht's voice would carry to those standing before him on the raised and tiered flooring.

At some point the interpreter must have tried to explain this complicated system of wers and bots to Augustine: the system seemed reasonable enough to him, for it was not unlike the one he had known among the Franks. He recited to Augustine some of the laws as he could remember them; he had attended the folk moot the day before, and heard the law declared in a marriage case: of such a law he doubted if a Christian could approve. 'If a free man,' he told Augustine, 'lie with the wife of another free man, he shall pay the husband his (or her) wergeld, and procure a second wife with his own money and bring her to the other man's home.'

'It is right,' said Augustine, 'that a man should pay heavily for such a sin, but it is wrong that he should buy another woman as if she were a slave, and it is wrong that a man can go on living with another man's wife, provided he pay the bot and find another wife for him whom he has thus defrauded. But the king's laws are for all men and very old. I shall not allow the converts to have another man's wife, while the first husband is alive.'

'You will have trouble, I think, Father, over these marriage customs,' said the interpreter, 'but what will happen to our people when they receive injuries?'

'Our Lord bids us turn the other cheek,' said Augustine.

'I know, Father,' said the interpreter, 'but one must be practical. The trouble is, that we, as foreigners and pilgrims, do not exist. We cannot ask for justice in the moot.'

Augustine considered this. 'It is true,' he said, 'we have no wer.'

'Moreover, Father,' said the interpreter, 'while the English people are just and require compensation for theft, no one knows how much compensation you should receive if a freeman or a slave steal a cup from your house or a gold chalice from the church.'

'A man dug through the wall of our barn last week,' said Augustine, 'and stole a side of bacon. The dean of the kitchen heard a noise in the night, and rose from his bed in the hall, and caught the thief as he was trying to drag the bacon through the hole he had made. I questioned the man, who was not a Christian, and I found his wife and children were hungry and indeed starving. I let him keep the bacon, and told him he had much better be baptised. I think he will come to baptism.

Unfortunately, his brother got into the sacristy two days later and stole a silver brooch which had been offered at the mass. Nor was he caught. One of the first thief's children told me.'

'Nothing you have will be safe, Father, if thieves think you cannot catch or punish them: and I do not see how you can do this.'

'I shall have to ask the king,' said Augustine, 'how much I am worth. And how much you are worth.'

The interpreter looked relieved, and even more so when Augustine added that all these laws should be written down, and in English, though this would be difficult, seeing that the English made such strange sounds in their talking.

However, in the end, the king agreed that Augustine's worth should be declared in the moot, and that all the laws of the Kentish people should be written down. 'If you can do it,' he said, 'I know that Latin can be written down, for I have seen it so written in the Cristes book you read from at mass. But I have never seen a book written in English, and I doubt if any man can write English down. Though my goldsmith made letters on my dagger sheath which meant that he had wrought it; or so he told me.'

'We have a young monk who is English born,' said Augustine; 'our Father Gregory bought him in the slave market in Gaul. He has been useful to me and I have had him taught to read and write Latin and made him an acolyte. I think he will be able to write the laws in English; for the English make sounds, though different ones from those we make in Italy. We write our sounds in letters; I shall tell the brother to write the English sounds in good capital letters, as in our choir books. It is well that the laws should be written down.'

'I do not see the need,' said Æthelberht, 'all men know them. But I can see that Christians like to have writings. So write them down, Father, and read them to me so that I know the writing is just; then you shall read them before me at the moot, and all men shall hear the wer that I have given to Christians, to you and the rest.'

The written laws of Æthelberht, as they have come down to us in manuscript, consist of a list of some ninety short clauses, headed: These are the decrees (dooms) that King Æthelberht made in Augustine's day. The reason for the writing, the need to fit the different grades of the clergy into the graded society of Englishmen, appears in the first clause:

> [Theft of] God's property and the church's shall be compensated twelve fold [twelve times the payment for theft of the same thing from a free man]; a bishop's property eleven fold; a priest's property nine fold; a deacon's property six fold; a clerk's property three fold. Breach of the peace shall be compensated doubly when it affects a church or a meeting place.

The next four clauses set down bots no doubt already well established: if a free man robs the king he shall pay back a ninefold bot, if the king feasts at anyone's house and any sort of an offence is committed there, a twofold bot shall be paid, etc. The bots for injury to the clergy and church property compare favourably even with offences against the king and royal property, and this was in line with Roman imperial law, which forbade clerks to bear arms and protected them from injury by heavy penalties.

The laws of Æthelberht, the first of the English law codes to be written down, were followed by the codes of the later Kentish kings and by the issue of a code by King Ine of Wessex (who reigned from 688 to 725). The fact that the Kentish laws were written in itself shows the influence of the Italian missionaries; but the forms of Roman law had no influence upon these early codes. They continued Germanic, understood by all men in the folk moot, and no class of professional lawyers developed to interpret them and comment upon them. On the Continent, notaries were professional legal scribes and jurists, but they were not employed in England, because their field of knowledge was different. Only the Church, from Archbishop Theodore's time (668–90), used notaries, and that to deal with canon law, which was written of course in Latin. The English kings themselves used their bishops or their palace chaplains later, to do such writing as they found necessary, whether for land grants, letters or additions to the law codes, which they themselves published in their moots or witans. Notaries they did not use; but bishops and particularly their deacons had knowledge of legal forms, notarial knowledge, if needed. Pope Gregory had seen to it that his own deacons had notarial training, and he even thought it fitting that professional notaries engaged for the most part on church work should be given a grade in the clerical militia, that of acolyte if they were married, or one of the holy orders if they were not. From Augustine's time onwards then the higher clergy may be assumed to have had some legal training, for they had all spent a year or two, some of them much longer, in the diaconate, and it was the deacon's business to write the bishop's letters and deal with the landed property of the bishop and his *familia*. The kings of Kent had the archbishop and his *familia* to assist them, the kings of Wessex the bishop and his *familia* in the Old Minster at Winchester. No royal notaries were needed; one reason why they were not needed was that the kings' new laws were written down by men whose ideas of justice were shaped, not only by the Christian scriptures, but by the principles of Roman law.

The code of Æthelberht has another point of interest: it dealt, on the royal authority, both with matters ecclesiastical and matters secular. This inclusion continued throughout the Anglo-Saxon period. The English Church used the diocesan synod for a bishop's administration of his diocese, and a provincial synod was rarely summoned (as in 787 to meet the papal legates); there were one or two provincial synods which issued codes of church law, in English, in the tenth and eleventh centuries. But normally laws about church matters were published on royal authority in the witan, even as theft from God's property was dealt with in Æthelberht's laws. It was of advantage to the archbishop to get such laws published in this way, made known to noblemen, thegns and freemen, and no sign of the church's subjection to the state. In the early codes the archbishop almost certainly drafted the ecclesiastical clauses himself, and quite possibly the whole code. Archbishop Wulfstan, much later, was a celebrated drafter of codes. The whole system of the publication of laws affecting ecclesiastical and secular matters equally by the king in his witan goes back to the work of Augustine at Durovernum.

One of Augustine's preoccupations in the short years of his episcopate was the building and care of churches. The monk-clergy must have an *oratorium* where they could pray, night and day; he, as bishop, must, as soon as possible, turn this *oratorium* into a worthy church, with an altar, his bishop's chair and a place for baptisms. In this church, where the chancel for the clergy should be marked off in some fashion from the main chamber, the king and his court could stand for mass, and for the long vigils that preceded the feasts, and for the baptisms. There should be a *diakonikon* if possible, and a chamber for the offerings, both opening into the church, and the church should be of stone.

Around Augustine's *mansio*, a timbered hall like the king's, stretched a city of wooden halls and plaster huts, some built alongside the old Roman streets, some above and across them. The Roman town plan was already lost, except for the walls. There was timber about, for the upper storeys of the Roman houses had been of timber, and there were plenty of Roman tiles and the thin Roman bricks; there were stone columns and capitals, lying tumbled alongside the old Forum. Augustine thought there would be material for churches, and one or two of his young monks could work stone and mix mortar; but he should get skilled masons if he could, from Gaul or Italy.

The churches he and his immediate successors built in Kent were on the Continental plan, and some remains still show signs of an Italian technique. The essentials for a small church were a rectangular chamber, for the congregation, and a semi-circular chancel, with the low stone altar on the chord of the apse. The old Roman church of St Martin in Augustine's time was small, some 14 feet in length, with thick walls of Roman brick and an apsidal end. The church of the Saviour (see p. 98) had nave and apsidal chancel, and side *porticus*, for *diakonikon* and offerings. The church of SS Peter and Paul, which Augustine planned for his monastery, was more elaborate, and its relation to the church of St Pancras, due east of the larger church, is not clear. Whether St Pancras's was completed before that of SS Peter and Paul, as a kind of interim church, while the larger one was a-building, or whether it was meant for public use while the monastic church was for the monks, is not known; it may even have existed before Augustine began the larger church, as an older Christian church or as a secular building. Its position suggests comparison with the churches at Glastonbury, where the successive churches were built on the same radial line to the east. The church of St Pancras had a nave 42 feet 6 inches by 26 feet 6 inches and its walls were built of Roman brick in a east. The church of St Pancras had a nave 42 feet 6 inches by 26 feet 6 inches and its walls were built of Roman brick in a pebbly mortar; between the apsidal chapel and the nave was a colonnade of four Roman columns, the space between the two central ones spanned by a brick arch, and that between the two outer sets of columns by lintels. Rather later, a *porticus* with external door was built outside the west door of the church, and a north and south *porticus* half way down the north and south sides of the nave. The church of St Pancras at Rome had lain near the monastery *ad clivum Scauri,* but the dedication here probably depended rather on the relics sent by Pope Gregory. A church with a similar ground plan was built for the monastery at Limynge, where Æthelberht's daughter came to be abbess after her marriage to King Edwin and his death in battle; this too had columns separating nave from the apsidal chancel.

Churches on a similar plan were built in the half-century after Augustine's death at Bradwell in Essex, the Roman coast fortress of Othona, and at Reculver, the Roman fortress of Regulbium. The church at Reculver was that in the minister built for the king's mass-priest, Bassa, in 669; it had nave, apsidal chancel, and north and south *porticus* overlapping the apsidal chancel; it had also three equal arches supported on columns dividing chancel and nave.

Durovernum in the Roman period lay securely inland, and defended by the forts of the Saxon Shore, Reculver, Richborough, Dover and Lympne, and with access by road or river to each. It is of interest that the Kentish kings should have had estates near the *termini* of these roads, and that they should have provided endowments for monasteries at Reculver, Dover and Lyminge (Lympne); and a little later not only at Dover, but at the other port into which the Watling Street branched, Folkestone. The connection between the landed estates of Æthelberht and his descendants with those of the Roman fisc has been earlier suggested.

The churches of all these early ministers or monasteries were thus on the same plan: an aisle-less nave, an apsidal chancel on the same level or but little raised, a colonnade generally with three pillars between them, and, as soon as they could be built, north and south *porticus,* generally adjoining or overlapping nave and chancel. The walls were thick, of Roman brick, or of flint and stone rubble with bands of Roman brick, the colonnade of stone, and the floors often of plaster coloured pink by an admixture of pounded Roman brick.

In view of the smallness and simplicity of these Kentish churches of the days of Augustine and his immediate successors, Augustine's abbey church of SS Peter and Paul must be reckoned a great church, a basilica reminiscent perhaps of old St Peter's on the Vatican Mount. Its ground plan was rectangular, with a central nave less wide than the two transepts and separated from the transepts (or north and south porticus) by a colonnade; the apse beyond the transepts was semi-circular and narrower than the nave. At the west end of the nave was a narthex and, on each side of the nave ,north and south porticus, for burials. The pulling down of the east end of the church by Abbot Wulfric later rendered exact knowledge of the east end of Augustine's church in any case unsure. Wulfric, in fact, joined by a rotunda Augustine's church and the little church of St Mary built of Roman brick to the east of, and on the same radial line as, St Augustine's. He thus made a fine Carolingian church like that of Saint Benigne at Dijon, but he made things difficult for the archaeologist investigating Augustine's church.

As was to be expected, Augustine's mission introduced the classical tradition to the English not only in building but in learning and book writing. The only book that survives to us from his day is one sent him by Gregory, of course not written and illuminated in England but in Italy: the illuminated manuscript of the gospels, Corpus Christi College MS 286. Palaeographers date this manuscript from the script as written in Italy in the mid-sixth century. When Augustine celebrated the mysteries, it would have stood upon the small, cube altar, and he would have read from it; in his day the only objects placed upon the altar were the chalice and paten and the gospel book. The gospel book in these days stood for Christ himself; indeed, in the library or chapel lists in the centuries following it is often entered as a 'Cristes boc'. One page of illuminations is ruled with lines dividing the space for a number of small pictures from the gospel, in the naturalistic manner. Other similar little pictures are painted into the book's great initial letters.

Though the school of illumination that grew up at Canterbury was never as famous as the northern schools, where the monks used for decoration all the Celtic patterns that had come down to them from the La Tene metal workers, yet the Canterbury school carried on the classical tradition of study and writing. No such outstanding example of illuminated book as the Lindisfarne gospels has come down to us from Canterbury; but there were some bad fires at Canterbury, one in the time of Lawrence, Augustine's successor, and manuscripts may have been lost then and destroyed or plundered in the ninth-century Danish raids. It is unlikely, however, that any such extravagantly beautiful books as the northern and Irish gospel books were ever produced at Canterbury: the *gravitas* of the classical tradition would not, without outside stimulus, lead to the production of such books. Under Archbishop Theodore, Canterbury was a centre of scholarship and learned lecturing: books must have been produced for the choir, the altar and the library: many and grave books, clearly written in uncials and half-uncials, rather than books whose illuminations would occupy the abbey's best scribe for so many weeks. In the matter of handwriting, however, the Irish, more angular form of the old Roman half-uncial script influenced Canterbury.

With regard to the books of secular learning and commentaries on the scriptures used at Canterbury in the century following Augustine it is difficult to be precise, for the works of no outstanding scholar in north or south Britain, from which the uses of particular sources could be ascertained, have survived completely. One long work of Archbishop Theodore remains to us, and some of his lectures on the scriptures, will, it is hoped, be published shortly. It is not likely, however, that Abbot Hadrian at Durovernum had a much less good library at his disposal than Bede at Jarrow, and Bede certainly had access to all the learned books in use in western Europe. We are told by Bede of the journeys his founder abbot, Benedict Biscop, made to the Continent, partly for the purpose of bringing back books and pictures; he did indeed bring back many books, but he had been abbot of St Augustine's abbey for two years before he founded his own monastery in the north, and it is possible that he desired to equip his own house with learned books such as Archbishop Theodore had already provided in Canterbury. It is possible that he ended by providing at Jarrow more and better books than could be found at Canterbury; but on the whole it is likely that the books Bede would have considered essential could also have been found at Canterbury. Bede was, for his day, an incomparable scholar, but his scholarship was partly the result of his leisure, his devotion to books and teaching: he had the leisure because he remained a simple monk, not necessarily because he had more books. At Canterbury, as at Jarrow, one may conjecture that by the time of Abbot Hadrian, they would have had the works of the great Latin theologians, especially those of Augustine and Gregory, Jerome's Latin scriptures and the commentators on them, and a number of the 'passions' of the martyrs and possibly some saints' lives; works on the monastic life, like those of Cassian, the Rule of the Master, the Rule of St Basil and, without straining probability, other more modern rules, including St Benedict's. They would almost certainly have the works of that great doctor, Isidore of Seville, the church history of Eusebius, and perhaps some of the works of Cassiodorus. But in Augustine's time, though Bede said Pope Gregory had sent him 'very many books', only the small nucleus of the library expanded under Theodore could have existed at Durovernum. It is not impossible that Pope Gregory should have chosen to send among them either the Rule of St Benedict, of which he spoke so highly, or even the Rule of the Master: so learned, so scriptural, and so terribly long. Its length must have been the great argument against its inclusion!

When Augustine had converted the king and baptised very many Kentish converts, there remained the task of providing for them the sacraments of the Christian life and opportunity to hear Christian teaching. The population of Durovernum, or even Kent, was to our mind, very small: but the churches Augustine could build were even smaller. It was scarcely to be expected that all the baptised Christians could have attended the Sunday mass celebrated at Christ Church, St Martin's and perhaps the little old Roman church under the modern St Peter's, or else the number of baptised Christians must have been very small indeed. But they would certainly be expected to be present at the great festivals of Christmas, Easter and Pentecost, the country people coming in from several miles around Durovernum and Durobrevis. Pope Gregory's advice that booths or some kind of shelter should be provided round the church, and oxen roasted to feed the people suggests that they did flock in at these times.

When the mind tries to picture the impact of the new missionaries on the Kentish peasant farmers and the king's court, these gatherings for feast days must have been a main point of contact. The new Christians would have had some instruction before baptism; they would be blessed by Augustine as he passed through them on the path from his dwelling to the church; they would see the monks in their long, dark clothes, one of them carrying the bishop's cross before him. Augustine was an elderly man, his dark hair and beard were growing grey, and they noticed that his head and his monks' were shaven. If they were lucky enough to get inside the church they would see Augustine and the monks, all now with long white linen garments over their black clothes, and Augustine had moreover a very splendid embroidered robe of silk, like a king's; it hung down in front and at the back and it had a cross in colour on the front. When Father Augustine prayed, his voice was like the bards' singing, and when the monks prayed, they too sang, those on one side of Father Augustine first, then those on the other. For when they came in, they passed through the people and under the arch, and the bishop had a seat in the midst of the farther chamber, behind the altar (they knew about altars: there were altars in the old sanctuaries of the pagans). The monks stood on each side of the bishop singing, and then the bishop stepped forward to the altar and began the prayers. All this while, and while the bishop prayed and read at the altar, they had been holding their offerings: some few of them a coin, or a piece of jewellery, or a dagger, and others eggs or a wildfowl they had snared or a bag of barley or wheat. One of the monks received the offerings (he too had a splendid silken dress) and carried them through the door in the altar place to the chamber of offerings.

Then the prayers became very solemn, and those that were in front and had room knelt; but generally they stood all through, being too tightly packed to kneel. And soon after that, all in this solemn silence, the men and women passed up to the altar, and to them, standing, the bishop gave the fair white bread which he had blessed; and this was indeed the paschal lamb and Christ himself. And to all of them in turn he gave the bread. . . .

The long teaching before baptism, the fine white bread of the mass at the feasts, the bishop's voice explaining the story he had read to them from Christ's book (when a man could get to mass on a Sunday), the marriage blessing, the baptism of his baby (for the bishop baptised all babies as well as full grown men and women at Easter and Whitsun, and anointed and blessed them); the getting the bishop to come and bless the cow when it fell sick, and his wife when she nearly choked with the coughing and fever in the bitter winter; the last prayers beside his old father when he died, and the prayers at his burying: in all these ways the life of the ceorl, or the noble, or the slave, touched Augustine as he tried to build up the church, and contend with the old pagans, at Durovernum.

The order of the mass he celebrated in his church on Sundays and the great feasts and the days of the martyrs were in the sacramentary book which he brought at his first coming: the only book beside those of the scriptures and the psalms. Afterwards, Pope Gregory sent him more books, perhaps yet another sacramentary. And yet, for most Sundays of the year the order of the mass being determined and the long prayer at the heart of it, the canon, remaining unchanged, the rest of the psalms and prayers and scripture readings lay at Augustine's discretion. The Sundays were, in the liturgical language of the day 'vacant'. A great deal, throughout the celebration, was thus customarily left to the discretion of the bishop; the ritual pattern of the liturgy, the eucharist, was fixed, but the celebrating bishop enjoyed a traditional freedom of phrasing, beyond the choice of introit, alleluia and communion psalms. Though Augustine must certainly have brought a sacramentary, there was no single, prescribed form of the mass prayers for use everywhere. Differing churches and localities had their own form of the rite, and Augustine, for the building up of the new church of the English, where there was no regional rite, had had special permission from Pope Gregory to borrow from the rites of other churches than the Roman whatever he deemed useful and appropriate.

He must have brought with him the current, Roman form of the Gelasian sacramentary, for this was a presbyteral sacramentary, the earlier Leonine, and the contemporary Gregorian sacramentaries both being pontifical ones. The Leonine and Gregorian, that is, had the order of the mass for the days the pope himself celebrated in the stational churches at Rome. The Gelasian sacramentary, on the other hand, was a parochial sacramentary; it had, besides the liturgical offices, many blessings useful in pastoral work. The Gregorian sacramentary, which may have reached Augustine at Durovernum during his episcopate, differed most notably from the Leonine and Gelasian in the order in which it recorded the succession of masses. Whereas the two earlier ones began with the Sundays of Advent and ended with Pentecost, the Gregorian calendar began on our New Year's Day and ended with the octave of Christmas, an arrangement found more and more convenient as time went on. But in all three of these sacramentaries the Sundays between Epiphany and Lent, and between Pentecost and Advent, were 'vacant'. The bishop on such Sundays might choose to celebrate one of a pool of special masses (in time of plague, for peace, for deliverance from enemies, etc.), or he might choose the psalms, collects and scripture readings as he would.

The question of the 'services' conducted by Augustine at the church of the Saviour, and, after his death, also at that of the monastery of SS Peter and Paul, is of interest; it has a bearing on the impact of Christianity on the eorls and ceorls and læts of Kent, and their wives. It is better understood in relation to the already centuries-old development of the liturgy in the west. In early days, and still in those of Augustine, worship for lay people was not a matter of a service early in the morning before the first meal, a service in the middle of the morning and one in the middle of the evening, or attendance at one or two of these. Worship in Augustine's day for the bishop's clergy, in Kent, in Ireland, in Gaul, Italy and everywhere else consisted of a night vigil, considerably shortened now for an ordinary Sunday but still a rather long pre-dawn and dawn service, leading up to the eucharist as its climax; this at least the laity would attend. The eucharist would be fairly early in the morning, before men had broken their fast, and on that Sunday there would be no more services, either 'morning' or 'evening'. The laity would rise early, according to their piety, attending more or less of the vigil service, get the bishop's blessing as he passed to and from the dawn service, and themselves crowd into the church or stand round outside, for the eucharist. The pattern of worship had evolved in the east, when the days were hot and the nights cool for prayer, and men's work was done; the assemblies of the early Christians were at night and the hour immediately following the dawn.

Speaking broadly, it was the monks, not the episcopal clergy, who began to worship together in the day-time, as a carrying out and translation into liturgical form of the precept: pray without ceasing [*orate sine intermissione*]. Not that the first attempt of the monks of the Egyptian desert to 'pray without ceasing' was liturgical: it was rather an attempt to pray continually in solitude, reciting the psalter or meditating over the scriptures with the minimum of intermission. Some hermits even refused to lie on a bed for sleep, but only allowed themselves to doze in a chair when they could no longer stay awake. This concept of continual prayer lay behind the gradual evolution of special hours of prayer, liturgical prayer, when monks began to live communally, as they did under Pachomius, partially, and under Basil, completely. The keeping of these hours of prayer extended through the day as well as the night. The episcopal clergy and the lay Christians had work in the day-time: they prayed in the cool darkness of the night (a time safer moreover for their assemblies before the persecutions were ended than the full light of day). The monks of Egypt living out in the desert as solitaries, making baskets perhaps to support life, but working for no man, could order the time of their occupation by day as well as by night. And when they came to live together under an abbot, he could dispose of their days as well as of their nights.

In the time of Gregory at Rome, and Augustine at Durovernum, it was the bishop and his clergy who celebrated the vigil and the eucharist that the laity attended. They were bound to celebrate as the *familia* of a bishop, as they would have done if Augustine had been a bishop and no monk; this was done in all the cathedral churches of Gaul or Italy. But since Augustine had once been a monk, and had been admonished in a letter of Pope Gregory that as a monk he could not live otherwise than communally with his clergy, it is likely that the monks, most of them with the monastic tonsure only, would continue the recitation of the day hours to which they were accustomed. It would be strange if Augustine never assisted at their offices, though he had now much pastoral work and royal business. But the laity, quite certainly, would not be expected to attend such offices, except the vespers before the great festivals and even before Sundays, such vespers having always been part of the original all-night vigil.[1] The pious among them might attend also the early dawn praises before the mass. (See for the early all-night vigil and offices, Appendix 2.)

If it is asked, what could the Latin offices and liturgy have meant to the Anglo-Saxon converts at Canterbury, it should be remembered that these people were familiar with the rites and sacrifices of their own priests, which by no means depended on reasoned discourses or admonitions to good living. There were, to the Cantware, powers beyond nature whose signs were seen in the sky and in men's lives; signs of divine pleasure in good crops from the fruitful earth, or the king's victory in battle; signs of displeasure in lightning and thunder, storms and tempests, the flooding of river banks, famine and pestilence. The priests, sacrificing to Thor and Woden, implored good fortune for the people, or allayed divine anger. The eorls and the ceorls, the læts and the serfs knew about the gods and had a sense of the holy: temples were holy, priests were holy, sanctuaries were holy, kings were holy, not as associated with virtue or justice, but as under the protection of the gods.

And now, as it seemed to many of the Cantware converts, the king had flouted the old gods and placed himself under the protection of this new god, the Saviour, whose priest was Father Augustine, who had a new temple and many servants. The king thought all this would bring good luck; but many of the eorls thought it would bring very bad luck. The king was getting old and won no more battles, and the priests of the great Harrow beyond Londinium and the other sanctuaries said he would die soon and there would be a new king, who would return to the old gods.

The Cantware converts, thinking thus, had no great certainty about the future, but they hoped for the best. They had made

---

[1] See for the pre-Carolingian and Carolingian development of the vigil and night office, C. Callewaert, J.C.D., *Archipresbyter . . . civitatis Brugensis: Sacris Erudiri: fragmenta liturgica collecta a monachis sancti petri de aldeburgo in steenbrugge ne pareant*, Steenbrugge 1940, a reprint of essays which appeared mainly between 1927 and 1932. See also A. Baumstark and P. O. Heiming in *Nocturna Laus Typen: frühchristlicher Vigilienfeier und ihr Fortleben vor allem im römischen und monastischen Ritus*, Münster Westfalen 1956.

the baptismal promises and they believed they would certainly go to the Saviour in his home in the bright heavens when they died, and this was a good thing. Meanwhile they remembered that Father Augustine said stealing was wicked, and they ought to help poor men and women and children, especially when they were homeless because the floods were out, or after a bad fire. Lying was a bad thing, and stealing another man's wife; but the folk law had always punished wife-stealing with a heavy fine. Fighting at the ale-house was bad too.

But it was a fine thing, and very holy too, to go to the vesper service when the sun sank, and see Father Augustine go into the new temple in his white linen robe, and hear his servants sing, one side answering the other across the temple in their strange wailing singing. There were even one or two Kentish boys with them now, living with Augustine in his hall and learning how to behave in a Christian way. There was even the son of an eorl. When he was sent on a message to one of the Kentish people the other day, he called the temple a 'church', which was some kind of a foreign word. He took the large cheese, which he had been sent for, back with him.

But the most interesting and the holiest thing for a Christian to do was to go to the *husel*, which was the Kentish word for sacrifice. The old priests offered sacrifices, and the Christian bishop naturally had his sacrifice. All the people round went at dawn and watched the bishop go into the 'church', and some followed him in, and he blessed them all when he came out, and they kissed his hands. And almost at once he came back again, wearing his mass hackle, a wonderful silk tabard, like the king's, over his white robe. All the people who could pressed in, and it was the Christian *husel*. There was no killing of an animal, but the bishop offered bread and wine upon the altar, and blessed them. It was all very holy and after the Christians had pressed into the church, or pressed round outside, they were very holy too, and had the Saviour's blessing. May it all turn out, the Kentish Christian said, for the best; and may the king defeat his enemies in war.

But for some of the new Christians baptism and the following of the Saviour meant more than this: more than the passing from the protection of the old gods to that of the god of the new foreign teachers, largely as showing loyalty to King Æthelberht, who had already done so. It was a savage age and the old gods had many supporters among the Anglo-Saxons, quite apart from their powers in thunder and storm and tempest. The new Church was to pass through a period of acute danger at Æthelberht's death, and if Augustine's converts had been, all of them, merely formal adherents of the new religion, the young Church could not have survived.

There were some who must have been struck by what Bede calls the 'blameless lives' of the new teachers, and wondered at the hard discipline under which they lived, and the lack of feasting and pleasure and wives and children; the king reckoned some of them as eorls by the wers he gave them, but they had none of the good things enjoyed by the eorls and the king's other servants. Rather, they seemed as theows, slaves, of Father Augustine and their god. They wondered at the healings granted to Father Augustine when he prayed to his god. They wondered at his words, when he spoke to them in the mass, bidding them pray for the sick, and explaining the words of the Cristes boc, which was laid upon the altar.

He said to them once that he was as a sower sent forth to sow his seed; that the Saviour made him scatter the seed over good land and bad land, in the fertile furrow and on the bare rock. That did not seem to them very good husbandry, for preparing the soil by the plough was great toil, and seed was precious; but the kindness of a sower who would do this, so that all men, good and bad, should be saved, was wonderful.

And it was more wonderful that the Saviour himself was as a shepherd, a good shepherd, Father Augustine said. He knew all his sheep by name; he knew his sheep were called Ecgfrith and Æthelwald and Sigeberht and Ceolwulf, yes, and Osthrith and Eanswithe and Eanflæd and Herelufa and Hild; he knew all their names. He was a brave shepherd, and if the wolves should come down upon his sheep from the woods above the south downs (where there are many wolves), he would fight them. Yes, Father Augustine said, he gave his life for the sheep. And the sheep, these Kentish Christians thought, might well be ready to give their lives for such a shepherd.

CHAPTER 7

# The Sequel to Augustine's Work

THE precarious nature of Augustine's standing in Kent is evidenced by the pagan reactions there, in the province of the East Saxons and in that of East Anglia, on the death of his protector, King Æthelberht. Augustine's death preceded that of Æthelberht by some years, and they were years of growing difficulty for the Christians. The power of the *bretwalda* over the subject kingdoms was military and unlikely to survive military defeat: and Æthelberht at his death was a very old man. He had been only a 'king's son', not a king, of Kent when the princess Bertha was sent over from Paris to marry him in 560; the Anglo-Saxon Chronicle says he succeeded his father Eormanric in 565; and he died in 616. A reign of fifty-one years is long for an Anglo-Saxon king, and the exact dates cannot be relied on, but Bede's account of how the king of the East Angles gained the leadership (*ducatum*) even in Æthelberht's own lifetime suggests that Æthelberht was then an ageing king.

Not only was Æthelberht now old and feeble, but Queen Bertha had died and Æthelberht had married again, apparently a young and beautiful woman, for when the old king died Archbishop Lawrence's influence could not prevent the new king Eadbald, Æthelberht's son, from marrying her himself. To marry a stepmother (*noverca*) was forbidden in canon law, but Christian influence at the Kentish court had waned. Bede suggests that the enormity of the offence brought upon him punishment from heaven and mental disturbance.

The storm threatening the Kentish Christians was increased by the death of King Saeberht of the East Saxons, whose three sons had persisted in their paganism. They had in their father's lifetime forborne to attend pagan rites, but now they began openly to worship idols themselves and give their people leave to do so. Apparently they were liberal enough in their views to attend the bishop's *husel*, as their father had, and they were affronted when the bishop would not give them the bread of the

108

eucharist, as he had done to their father: 'Why', they said, 'do you not hold out the fair white bread to us as you did to Saba our father?' For thus they were wont to call him. And the bishop said to them: 'If your will is to be washed in the font of salvation, as your father was, you may share this holy bread which your father shared; but if you scorn the laver of life, you can by no means avail to share in the bread of life.' But they said, 'We will not enter that font, for we know that we have no need of it: yet we will indeed be fed with that bread.' And when Bishop Mellitus had many times admonished them and said that no man might communicate in the sacred offering unless he had been cleansed in the holy washing, they became extremely angry. 'If you will not assent to our petition then, seeing it is one so easy to grant, you can no longer dwell in our dominions.' And they drove him out and commanded him to leave their kingdom with all his followers.

Mellitus, therefore, left Londinium and went to Kent to talk with Lawrence the archbishop and Justus, bishop of Rochester, and they jointly decided that it was better for them all to return to their own country where they might freely serve God, than to live among barbarians who were rebels to the faith, where their work could bear no fruit. So Mellitus and Justus withdrew to Gaul, leaving Lawrence at Canterbury for the time being. But those kings who had expelled them were not left long to serve in the worship of demons, for they went forth into battle against the men of Wessex and they perished, together with all their forces. But though the leaders of the pagan reaction were dead, the people whom they had stirred up to these ill deeds could not be corrected and recalled to the simplicity of that faith and love which is in Christ. The sees of Londinium and Durobrevis remained for a time vacant.

At Durovernum, however, where the Christian church was older and stronger, and where Augustine slept in the church in the monastery dedicated to the blessed apostles Peter and Paul, Lawrence still lingered, unwilling to follow Mellitus and Justus across the Channel. He had his bed laid in the church of the monastery and in the night he poured out prayers and tears for the state of his church: and he slept, and St Peter came and scourged him for thinking that he, as a shepherd, could flee and leave his flock in such danger. And when next morning he showed the stripes of the scourging to King Eadbald, the king marvelled that the bishop should have suffered these things at the hands of the apostle; and at length he renounced the worship of idols and his unlawful marriage. He received the faith of Christ and when he was baptised he was careful to give his counsel and favour in all church matters, in so far as he could.

He sent to Gaul and recalled Mellitus and Justus and bade them build up again their churches in Londinium and Duro-brevis. Justus indeed returned to the city of Hrof, of which he was bishop, but the people of Londinium would not receive back their bishop, for (as Bede says) they preferred to serve idols rather than bishops. For King Eadbald's power was less great than his father's had been, to protect the bishop of the East Saxons at Londinium against the will of the pagans. But in his own kingdom, and among his own people from among whom he had been converted to God, he was studious to obey the divine commandments. And in the monastery of SS Peter and Paul, to the east of the main church and on the same radial line he built the church of the holy mother of God, and Bishop Mellitus when the time came consecrated it.

For in King Eadbald's reign Archbishop Lawrence died, he who had come over with Augustine and gone back to Gregory, asking for more help to build up the Church of the English. He died on 2 February 619, and he was buried near his master and predecessor Augustine in the church of the monastery; and Bishop Mellitus of London became the third archbishop of Durovernum, or as men were now beginning to call the city, Cantwarabyrig, the fortress of the Cantware. For the walls of the old Roman city still stood, and the Watling Street passed through it down to the ford; but the roads of the old city were now mainly lost, covered by the wooden halls, the small lath-and-plaster buildings and the new trackways of the city of the Cantware. But the church of the Saviour and the church of the monastery were of stone and the latter church was indeed a burial church for the kings of Kent and their archbishops; King Eadbald himself was buried there, beside his father and Queen Bertha, when he died in April 624.

Bede records no correspondence between the pope at Rome and Archbishop Lawrence, but he does relate that Pope Boniface IV wrote 'letters of exhortation' to his successor

Mellitus, who ruled the Church of the English with much care and toil. He was infirm of body, being troubled with arthritis, but whole in mind, ever in mind leaping from earthly things and passing swiftly to those heavenly things which he sought. As one instance of his virtue, Bede said, he mentions Mellitus's conduct when a great fire threatened his church at Durovernum. It seemed as if the whole city would be devoured by the flames sweeping over it, for the water thrown on them availed not to stop them. The bishop, trusting in divine aid, for indeed there was no human help, commanded himself to be placed in the path of the flames, where they raged around him and pieces of timber fell past his head. For men placed him in that place where the savage onslaught of the flames was greatest, by the martyrium of the Four Crowned Martyrs. And when he had been borne thither by his attendants, the sick bishop began by prayer alone to beat down the flames, a thing which the strength of a band of toilers had been unable to do. For without delay the wind which was blowing from the south and spreading the flames over the city veered round, and turned its furious onslaught away from the buildings which had lain in its path, directing its flames on the part of the city already burnt so that they were forced to die down. For the man of God was so filled with the flame of divine charity that his prayer availed to make the powers of the air and the winds in the sky obey him.

That other companion of Augustine, the Bishop Justus of Rochester, succeeded Mellitus as archbishop; and he consecrated the priest Romanus, from the minster of the princess Æthelburga down at Lyminge, to be bishop of Rochester. Lyminge lies on a royal estate of the Kentish kings to the north-west of Folkstone, and Romanus gave his name to the people living in the marshland between the Lemanan river and the south coast; they were called in his day the Rumining *seta* or Romanus's people, or the Merscwara, dwellers in the marsh. And now he was moved up north to where Justus had built his bishop's church at Durobrevis on the Medway.

To Justus the archbishop Pope Boniface IV writes on his accession, saying he has received letters from the king of Kent (whose name he gets wrong), speaking of the conversion of King Eadbald and his people. Knowledge of Justus's accession must have come from this letter. The pope commends Justus for his toils, and exhorts him to persevere to the end, when he shall receive the reward due to one through whom it has been made true of the apostles, that 'their sound is gone out to all lands and their words to the ends of the earth'. He sends Justus the pallium and licence to wear it in celebrating the sacred mysteries only, granting him also the right to ordain bishops (alone) as opportunity demands and the mercy of God grants grace, so that the conversion of the unconverted may be hastened. And may he use these rewards conferred on him for the good of souls, so that he be not charged with their misuse before the tribunal of the great and terrible judge, at his coming; and may God keep him safe.

So much for the companions of Augustine and successors in his see. Justus lived for thirty years after the original coming, and died in 627. Of his successor, Honorius, we know nothing previous to Bede's mention of him as archbishop. Though he used a Latin name, as did his successor Deusdedit, it would seem that he must have been one of the Anglo-Saxon boys received at Durovernum for training in the archbishop's *familia*; there is time for him to have received the priesthood in the years between 597 and 627. It was normal at Rome at the time for boys and young men to receive a new name at their entry to the clerical or monastic order, and contemporary Mediterranean practice still prevailed at Canterbury. After the episcopate of Deusdedit, and the longer rule of the Greek Archbishop Theodore at Canterbury (?668–90), all the English bishops and archbishops retained their Anglo-Saxon names: Berhtwald, Tatwine, Nothelm, etc. We do not know Honorius's Anglo-Saxon name, but it is likely that he was English.

Though in Augustine's lifetime the faith spread no farther than the south-east corner of England, the region where Æthelberht's protection was strong, and though Augustine's negotiations with the British bishops failed, yet in the days of his companions the church of Canterbury extended her mission and the schism with the Celtic Christians was ended. The church of Canterbury sent the missionary bishop, Paulinus, northward to Deira (Yorkshire), and knowledge of the faith as held by Christians in the Mediterranean was extended to the northern Christians taught by Iona. Not that the two churches held the faith differently, but their ecclesiastical practice differed, the Celts following an older and in the main a Gallic usage. Now the two groups of Christians with their differing practice were brought nearer together.

If it is asked, why did Augustine fail to win acceptance of his proposals from the Welsh abbots and bishops, though he had been sent by the Petrine see, whereas the authority of that see was in fact accepted by the Celts at the synod of Whitby in 664? the answer must be: because Augustine was negotiating, not with a king, but with the Celtic spiritual leaders themselves; whereas Wilfrid and his bishop and Paulinus's deacon, James, were trying to win over a king, and a king of the northern Angles at that. He could make his choice about acceptance of the Celtic or Roman obedience effective. There was no king at Augustine's Oak or at the synod near Bangor; but there was a king, a king of Anglian stock but taught his religion by the northern Celts, to settle the matter at Whitby. He did settle it: and his own court bishop, Colman, refused to accept such a settlement, and went back with his followers to Scotland. And King Oswiu's decision stood.

The years between Augustine's death and the synod of Whitby were years of hard work for the spreading of the faith, both by Augustine's church at Canterbury and Columba's monastery of Iona; and indeed, by missionaries from the Franks, from Ireland, and by an occasional effort by the Roman see to help on the conversion of the Anglo-Saxons. Among the several English kingdoms the best chance was probably in the north, for Christianity had lingered long in the region north and south of Hadrian's Wall, even sending Ninian to convert the Picts north of the Wall, and Patrick to convert the Celts of Ireland. From the Bangor (monastery) in northern Ireland, and from that of Moville, came Columba and his Scots, across the northern Channel; they founded Iona and converted the Picts of 'Scotland'. They spoke a language not very different from that of the conquered Britons of Northumbria, whose long and bitter defence of their country from the Angles who settled at Tyne-mouth and along the coast had led to a settlement relatively favourable to the northern Britons. The Celtic element in the population, that is, was much more numerous than in Kent, where the Romano-British population largely fled to the west or to Brittany, or remained as the social inferiors of the Anglo-Saxons, the conquered læts. The invading Angles in Northumbria established their kings and their rule, but there was social mixture of the two peoples. The art forms on the ornaments of the northern kings were Celtic, not Germanic. The northern Angles, after the victories of their pagan king, Æthelfrith (592–616), were not violently hostile to their northern neighbours and their Christian religion.

It was the Angles of Deira, however, whose king became *bretwalda* on the death of Rædwald of east Anglia, who were the first to accept Christianity, and from the south. King Edwin sought honourable marriage with Æthelberht's daughter, Æthelburga, and she was sent to him in 625 with the stipulation that she should remain Christian. Archbishop Mellitus consecrated Paulinus to be her chaplain bishop. Nor did Edwin refuse to consider becoming Christian himself, at the time these arrangements were made, but he said he would have to consider the matter with his witan. He was very learned for a seventh-century Anglo-Saxon king, whose main function was the leading of his armies in battle; someone at his court had read to him Vegetius on the art of war, and he had certain customs, which he believed Roman, copied at his court. He was aware of the glory of the Roman name, and of another world across the Channel where the Romans and their learning and their customs were better remembered; he desired to have as his wife a princess who was well educated and whom no one could call ignorant or barbarian. As to being a Christian, he would see about it. Meanwhile, he had an honourable letter from Pope Boniface (IV), and so had his queen Æthelburga, one in which the pope exhorted her at length to win her husband from the detestable errors of darkness to the Christian faith.

This indeed happened: Edwin defeated his enemy, the Northumbrian king Æthelfrith, in the battle of the Idle, down on the borders of Mercia, and accepting Paulinus's counsel, summoned a council to debate with him the acceptance of Christianity. Coifi, the pagan priest, himself advised it, saying the gods he had served were powerless, and an old councillor, in a famous speech, compared our life to the flight of a bird through a chieftain's lighted hall, from one darkness to another; if the new teaching could tell anything certain about the brief mystery of our life, let it be followed. Seeing there was no hostility from his people, Edwin was baptised at York, at the Easter ceremonies of 627. His headquarters were at Malton, in east Yorkshire; but Paulinus clearly remembered Pope Gregory's letter of advice to Augustine. The metropolis of the old Roman province had been at York, and there should a Christian bishop build his see church, that it might, when faith in the north had been extended, become again a metropolitan see. And there indeed, knowing the little wooden oratory in which Edwin had been baptised insufficient, Paulinus and Edwin set about building a more splendid basilica of stone, enclosing the original oratory within it. They had the foundations dug for a square, centrally planned church; but the building of a stone church by those accustomed only to building with wood took time, and before the walls of the basilica at York were risen to their full height, in a short six years that is, King Edwin was defeated and killed by the united force of his enemies at the battle of Hatfield, in the year 633.

But these six years were important for the future of the English Church, for Paulinus's work in them perpetuated the Gregorian plan for a metropolitan see at York, rather than at Lindisfarne, which for many years must have seemed the more likely. News of the apparently sure foundation of the church at York must have reached Pope Honorius, and certainly a letter from King Edwin requested the honour of the pallium for his bishop Paulinus. In June 634 the pope sent a formal letter to Edwin saying that he rejoiced in the king's deliverance from error and the integrity of his Christianity, known to all the world. He exhorted the king to bear in mind with frequent reading the doctrine of 'him who was your preacher, my lord Gregory of apostolic memory', that 'his prayers may extend your people and your kingdom and present you without reproach to almighty God. . . . And those powers that you hope for in the ordaining of bishops, such powers as a reward for the sincerity of your faith which has been by the manifold account of the bearers of this present letter [Edwin must have sent messengers who conferred with the pope and were then returning with his letter] we have arranged to grant you freely and without delay; for we have directed two pallia, one for each of the two metropolitans, to be sent to them, that is to Honorius and

Paulinus; so that when either of them shall be summoned to pass from this world to his creator, he shall be empowered by this our authority to ordain another bishop in his place.'

Pope Honorius shows in this letter, by his reference to Gregory, apostolic both as holder of the apostolic see and as the preacher of the faith to the English, that he knows the Gregorian authority for the setting up of a metropolitan see at York, and that he knows also the fewness of bishops among the English. He allows either metropolitan, when he knows death approaching, to ordain a successor to himself—a dispensation which Gregory had himself conceded to Augustine. Though Edwin was, indeed, killed in battle and the pagan Penda ruled a conquered Northumbria before the pallium arrived, yet Honorius's action had in fact recognised York as a metropolitan see. Paulinus received his pallium in Kent, where he had brought Queen Æthelburga to save her from the pagan conquerors of Deira. If he wore his pallium at mass, and there was no reason why he should not do so for the pallium was a personal honour, he wore it only at the minster of Lyminge, or the see church at Rochester. He was never able to return to York.

Bede speaks with some admiration of the work of Paulinus in his six short years in the north. He baptised Edwin's two boy children by his first wife, and the three children born to Edwin and Æthelburga. They died young and were buried in the church at York. He baptised many nobles and freemen of the king; he went with the king soon after his baptism to the royal hall of Yeavering in the extreme north and spent a month and more there, catechising and baptising. Yeavering, which lay in the part of Northumbria beyond Hadrian's Wall, had a royal hall and halls also for the nobles, all built of wood; it had one hall apparently earlier used in a pagan cult, and then for the Christian rites; its cemeteries had pagan and Christian burials. Not only did Paulinus thus baptise in Bernicia, the northern-most of the two Northern kingdoms, but throughout Deira as well; he baptised in the river, for there were as yet no churches or oratories; Bede says specially that he baptised in Swaledale, in the river that flows by Catterick. And where the king had a royal hall at Campodunum (near Huddersfield) he built a basilica of wood, with a stone altar; afterwards, the pagans who killed King Edwin in battle burnt the church, all but the altar, which the fire could not touch. Later kings built for themselves another hall at Leeds.

So great a devotion also had King Edwin to the faith that he persuaded Earpwald, king of the East Angles and son of King Rædwald, to abandon his pagan idols and embrace it. King Rædwald had indeed, in Augustine's time and while he acknowledged Æthelberht as over-king, received the Christian sacraments, but not whole-heartedly; for when he got back home his wife and certain pagan teachers seduced him from the sincerity of the faith. Like the Samaritans of old, who reverenced both Christ and their own old gods, Rædwald in the same temple had an altar made for the sacrifice of Christ and a little altar where sacrificial victims could be offered to demons. Bede said that the king of the East Angles in his own day had seen this temple which was then still standing. Bede knew nothing of the finding in our day of the great burial ship at Sutton Hoo, on the southern borders of East Anglia, nor of how the Christian king in whose honour it was raised was buried elsewhere near a Christian church, while the space for his body in the ship's centre was left clear, surrounded by a great treasure of arms, silver bowls, brooches, a war standard and an ox's head on a great silver platter. Bede would not have been surprised however; he knew that pagan cults had survived in East Anglia long after the king and the royal family had embraced Christianity.

Not only did Paulinus and Edwin convert Earpwald of East Anglia, but Paulinus preached much in Lincolnshire, the province intermediate between Edwin's own kingdom of Deira and East Anglia. First of all he converted Blaecca, king's reeve of the city of Lindum (Lincoln), together with his household, and he had built there in the city of Lindum a stone church of very fine work. The walls were still standing in Bede's day, though the roof had fallen, either through long neglect or because an enemy had thrown it down; but in this fine stone church at Lincoln, Paulinus, on the death of Archbishop Justus, consecrated Honorius to be archbishop of Canterbury.

We hear little enough, in Bede's stately narrative, of the pastoral work of Augustine and his companions; he had too long a story to tell and personal anecdotes that might have delighted a modern reader were scarcely in the Latin tradition.

But he does record (on the authority of Abbot Deda of Partney, a most truthful man, who had it from an old man baptised at mid-day with a crowd of other candidates by Paulinus in the river Trent, in the presence of King Edwin himself), that Paulinus was a tall man, rather stooping, with black hair and a thin, ascetic face, his nose slender and aquiline: he was both venerable and awe-inspiring to look at. He had to help him in administering baptism to this crowd James, his deacon, who worked very hard and was a man very noble in Christ. Bede tells us that when Paulinus had to take ship with the queen and sail down the coast and past Thames mouth to the Stour and Canterbury, he left James to look after the Christians who had been so short a time baptised. He stayed there, apparently with no priest to help him, for some thirty-one years, from Edwin's defeat and death in 633 till the synod of Whitby in 664. He shepherded and prayed with his people and he taught the Christian boys to sing the psalms of the office, all in the Gregorian chant, singing from memory, through the long years when the great warlike heathen, King Penda, lorded it over Mercia, his own land, and also over Northumbria and Deira. But Penda's son, the prince Peada, had received the Christian faith and sacraments in 653, years before his father's death, together with many of his people; he then married a Christian princess from Northumbria so that James and his converts were not left alone all this time, unprotected under a heathen king; there were Christians baptised by Paulinus and encouraged by Peada, who was converted either by the southern-trained Christians of East Anglia or by James himself; and there were the Northumbrian princess and her attendants, trained by the Celtic Christians. There was a difference of observance in Mercia as well as in the northern court. To James, now an old man, it must have seemed a minor matter compared with the hostility of pagans and Christians.

The peace with the Celtic Christians, for which Augustine had struggled (it is not likely to have seemed a matter of much importance to his protector Æthelberht), was now near at hand. The real difficulty, the acceptance by the Celts of their conquerors' religion, and the reconciliation of two very different Christian ways of life, was to be discussed by theologians as if it were merely a difference about the way of determining the dating of Easter.

The Celtic Christians, in western Britain, Scotland and Ireland followed traditions that had developed in a Christian, tribal society. Their clergy were monastic, their abbots often the sons of tribal kings, they had no 'cities' like those of the old west Roman empire, and consequently no territorial bishops. They had the Christian scriptures and the Christian sacraments and the tradition of monastic holiness that had come to them ultimately from Egypt: and perhaps mediately from the monasteries of Tours and Lérins. Their lands, Ireland and Scotland, had never been Romanised, and the western fringes of Britain, Cornwall, Somerset, Wales, Cumberland, had been only lightly Romanised; their laws were the old tribal laws, not Roman law, and though in their monasteries in the seventh century there were some manuscripts other than those of the scriptures, some Latin learning, it was very tenuous compared with that of the countries round the Mediterranean. Their Church was missionary, and their form of the Christian life had a certain freshness and simplicity as practised in a primitive, peasant society; their calendar and liturgy were Gallican rather than Italian, and somewhat old-fashioned owing to the interposition of a pagan Anglo-Saxon wedge in the sixth century between them and Europe. But they conceived of themselves as a Christian church like the other Christian churches, and all of them as part of the one, catholic and apostolic Church of the creed. Where their practice differed from that of the men from Canterbury, they justified it as apostolic.

When Augustine had met the Welsh bishops, a large tract of pagan country had intervened between the Celtic Christians and those of the Roman and Mediterranean tradition at Canterbury: Augustine was concerned to carry out Pope Gregory's instructions, but the problem of Christians living under different traditions in the same area was not acute. By the mid-seventh century, however, it was becoming acute. Missionary efforts from both sides had made it so.

East Anglia had a royal house converted by a king (Sigeberht) who had learned his religion in Gaul and assisted the Burgundian bishop Felix in the conversion of his subjects. He was killed in battle by Penda in 634; but Anna, his successor, was a pious king with a pious family; two of his daughters became nuns and one married a king of Kent who ordered his subjects to destroy all idols and keep the Lenten fast. The East Anglian kings were in touch with Kent and Canterbury; but, on the other hand, they protected also the Irish missionary, St Fursey, who worked from Cnobheresburg, his monastery near Yarmouth. Since both sets of Christians were protected by the king, and lived in different regions, their different dates for Easter caused little inconvenience.

The West Saxons, again, had been converted, with their king, by the Gallic missionary bishop Birinus, c. 635; but they had memories of a Celtic saint, St Cyngar, who had had his llan or monastery at Congresbury a century earlier; and they had as neighbours the Celtic Christians of Devon and Cornwall, with the age-old monastery of Glastonbury (Yniswitrin).

Mercia, as has been said above, had only a struggling Christian Church, which looked to East Anglia as its founder; it adjoined Deira, with its struggling group of Christians, and over against them both to the north lay Bernicia, which by the mid-seventh century followed the Celtic religious tradition under King Oswald. Oswald was destroyed by the heathen Penda at Maserfield in 642; but when his son Oswiu achieved the defeat of Penda in 654, he too ruled Northumbria as a Celtic Christian, inspired by memories of Iona and Bishop Aidan. But to strengthen his right to rule the kingdom of Deira as well as Bernicia, he married Eanflaed, daughter of King Edwin, and she had been baptised by Paulinus and long followed the Latin tradition in Kent. She had been taken there as a child when Paulinus rescued her mother from the conquering Mercians. King Oswiu now found himself following a different tradition and calendar from his wife. The practical difficulties arising from the following of the two traditions in one social group, present by now in nearly all the Anglo-Saxons kingdoms, were crystallised at his court. As Bede remarked, Easter had at times to be celebrated twice at Oswiu's court, for the king might have finished the Lent fast and be celebrating Easter Sunday, while the queen and her attendants were still fasting and keeping the day of palms.

It is curious that Oswiu, with all the traditions of Iona, his heroic father, and the gentle and saintly Aidan behind him, should have decided (as modern historians believe) before he summoned the great ecclesiastical synod of Whitby to give his decision to put himself under the protection of the Petrine see and the observance of the church of Canterbury. It points to his ability to appreciate that the 'catholic Easter' was in fact the Easter of the greater part of Christendom: that to profess belief in the catholic Church, as of course all the Celtic Christians did, should logically entail sharing the catholic observance under the church of the prince of the apostles. It points also to the fact that there was no such bitter hostility between the Christians taught by Iona and those of Canterbury as between the Welsh Christian leaders and the church of their conquerors.

Bede describes the debate at Whitby as focused on this question of the right dating of Easter. Colman, Oswiu's bishop, asserted that they followed the dating system of their fathers, which was that of the apostle John: it was, he claimed, apostolic. Wilfrid, once the pupil of Lindisfarne and now long versed in the learning and the canons of Gaul and Rome, claimed that the Easter his party celebrated they had seen at Rome, where the blessed apostles Peter and Paul lived, taught, suffered and were buried; it was Easter as kept in Italy, Gaul, Africa, Egypt, Greece and the whole world where Christ's Church had spread. It was the catholic Easter.

Modern scholars, and especially the Bollandist, Paul Grosjean,[1] have pointed out about Bede's account of the debate at Whitby that the 'computus' or dating rule debated there, and now held, did not, in fact, go back to the council of Nicaea. 'Easter is the Sunday which follows the fourteenth day of the moon which attains this age on the 21st March or immediately after.' The first scholar to attribute this rule to the council of Nicaea was, in fact, Dionysius Exiguus, the Scythian and Greek-speaking monk who was consulted by the secretariat of the Roman Church in 526 about the right date for keeping Easter. The Roman Church thereafter did not feel herself bound in all circumstances to follow this rule; but it was the rule normally followed at Rome in the time of Gregory and Augustine, and about three years after the synod of Whitby Pope Vitalian, writing to King Oswiu, attributed the 'apostolic' rule expressly

[1] 'La date de Pâques et le Concile de Nicée', in the *Bulletin de la classe des Sciences*, 5<sup>e</sup> Série, XLVIII (1962) of the Académie royale de Belgique, pp. 55–66.

to the Fathers of Nicaea. Bede was right in not giving full credence to the assertion of Dionysius that the Easter rule had been laid down at Nicaea; but he or the disputants at Whitby was or were mistaken in discussing the practice of the 'Quartodecimans' as a live issue. The Quartodecimans had indeed kept Easter on the fourteenth day of the month, regardless of whether or not it was a Sunday, but at a period long anterior to the council of Nicaea. No church in Britain in 664, Celtic or otherwise, was in fact Quartodeciman. This was already a practice lost in antiquity.

'Tell me, Colman,' said Oswiu after long disputation of the cycles that should or should not be used for the Easter computus, 'were the words: "Thou art Peter and upon this rock I will build my church. . . . I will give to you the keys of the kingdom of heaven," indeed spoken by the Lord to Peter?'

'They were indeed,' Colman replied.

'And can you allege any such weighty words as spoken to your Columba?' said the king.

'No. None,' answered Colman.

Then Oswiu declared that he would by no means gainsay the heavenly gatekeeper, lest when he came himself to the heavenly kingdom he who held the keys should turn away from him and refuse to unlock the gate. And all who sat in council with him agreed with the king, great and small alike; and, in Bede's words, having learned of the better observance, they abandoned the less perfect. From that time, Englishmen kept one Easter, reverenced the bishop in his territorial see, and fused together in their monasteries the treasures of Mediterranean and Celtic art and learning. There was no longer any fatal obstacle to Pope Gregory's plan for the setting up of two provinces with metropolitan sees. Augustine's work was completed.

There was, however, a sequel to this adherence to the Gregorian observance at Whitby in 664. Augustine slept at Canterbury and the English clergy never forgot it; it was, as it were, the sign and pledge of the patronage of their church by St Gregory, its founding father. Neither at Rome nor at Canterbury was knowledge of Pope Gregory's plan for the episcopate allowed to lapse, though for a time the claim of York as metropolitan was endangered, and later, in the reign of Offa, that of Canterbury.

The see of York had been long vacant when Oswiu accepted the Roman claims at Whitby: the kings of Northumbria, Christian since Oswald, had no concept of a territorial episcopate, and their bishops, Aidan, Finan and Colman had their sees in the monastery of Lindisfarne, conveniently near to the king's court at Bamburgh. When Colman refused to accept Oswiu's decision at Whitby and returned to Iona, Tuda, taught by the southern Scots, became Oswiu's bishop, but soon died of the plague that swept England in the summer of 664. Oswiu then appointed Eata, one of the pupils of Aidan, bishop of Lindisfarne; he had the episcopal charge in Bernicia, sometimes setting his chair in the church of Lindisfarne, sometimes in that of Hexham. Like Colman before him, he lived like a Celtic saint, travelling with a few clerks and in every village to which he came collecting the people, preaching, catechising, baptising and healing the sick; he would accept neither money nor beasts from any man, and he would not even accept land or possessions for the building of monasteries, unless he were compelled by the powers of the world. The villagers of Bernicia, accustomed to the ministry of the travelling Celtic monk priests, flocked to hear him.

Bede, however, says nothing of his pastoral care as extending to Deira, where Oswiu's son, Alchfrid, was under-king to his father, and where such villagers as were Christian had had teachers from the south and east. The see of York had been long vacant, and Peada sent the priest Wilfrid to Gaul to seek consecration. He sent him to the Frankish bishop Agilberht, his old master, now bishop of Paris, and Agilberht received Wilfrid with honour, summoned several Frankish bishops to assist him in the consecration, and ordained him bishop most honourably in the royal vill of Compiègne. All this took a little time, and while Wilfrid lingered across the Channel by reason of the consecration, Oswiu, 'imitating his son's industry' sent to Kent for ordination a holy man called Chad. He was modest in demeanour and way of life, and sufficiently instructed in holy scripture, and what he learned in scripture should be done, he prudently carried out; now Oswiu sent him to be made bishop of the church in York. Now the plague had been ravaging England and when Chad reached Kent, he found that Archbishop Deusdedit had died, and no other bishop had as yet

succeeded him. So he turned aside to the province of the East
Saxons, where Wine was bishop. Wine, who, as Bede said elsewhere, had bought his see of London from Wulfhere, king of
the Mercians, consecrated Chad, two British bishops who still
celebrated Easter uncanonically assisting him. There was no
bishop canonically ordained in Britain at the time other than
Wine, but to have received ordination from a simoniac was most
unfortunate. Chad was a holy man whose humility and modesty
Bede stresses; but the consecration of a metropolitan bishop, who
should himself ordain other bishops, by a simoniac and two
claustral bishops, even in an emergency, was likely to be
regarded as doubtfully sufficient. We do not know who the two
British bishops were: even the sees of St David's and Bangor
were monastic rather than territorial, and records could not be
produced to show when and by whom the first bishops of these
sees were consecrated.

Wilfrid then returned from Gaul, most canonically consecrated and ready to rule the churches of the Angles in all the
details of catholic observance, to find Chad accepted by
King Oswiu as his bishop, and as bishop of York. Archbishop Theodore, when he came to Canterbury from Rome,
re-ordained Chad and vindicated Wilfrid's claim to the see of
York. Chad was sent to be bishop of the Mercians. But in 678
Wilfrid was driven from York by King Ecgfrith of Northumbria, and Archbishop Theodore divided the great Northumbrian diocese, without reinstating Wilfrid. The long
struggle between Wilfrid and Theodore followed, the holder
of the York see never in fact holding metropolitan rank. While
the kings of Northumbria in fact ruled from Bernicia and the
north, it was difficult for the king's chief bishop to have his see
in York, the centre of an under-kingdom. Nor was Archbishop
Theodore willing to complicate a difficult situation by sup-
porting Wilfrid, who was unacceptable to the Northumbrian
kings. Not till the pontificate of Archbishop Egbert (732–66)
did the archbishop of York exercise all the metropolitan powers
of the head of a province, as indicated by Pope Gregory in his
letter to Augustine.

The question of the maintenance of the two provinces of the
Gregorian scheme was to be connected with the renewed

interest of the papacy in English affairs in the eighth century. The English Church devoutly commemorated each year her conversion by Pope Gregory through Augustine his servant; archbishops received, at their own request or that of the king who reckoned the archbishop his counsellor, the pallium which had become the characteristic sign of their office; pilgrims visited the basilica that covered the place where St Peter lay buried; but there was no regular administrative contact between the English Church and the papacy. When Wighard, King Oswiu's candidate for the see of Canterbury, had been sent to Rome for consecration and had died there, Pope Vitalian had chosen and consecrated Theodore as archbishop, and thus by his choice inaugurated one of the most constructive periods in the building up of the English Church. The papacy twice received the appeals of Bishop Wilfrid against Theodore, recorded them in its registers, and gave its support to Wilfrid; the king who disliked the decision would not deny the apostolic right to decide, but declared that these particular apostolic letters must be forgeries. In the end, Archbishop Theodore made peace with Wilfrid.

It was through the work of the Englishman Boniface for the conversion of Germany and a general church reform that the ties between the English Church and the papacy were strengthened. Boniface had been consecrated bishop for his mission work by the pope, and in all his efforts for the holding of synods to promote reform he acknowledged his commission from the see of Peter and urged subjection to the holy see together with the reform of abuses. When, through his influence, the reforming synod of Clofeshoh was held in 746, proceedings were opened by the reading of a letter from 'the pontiff venerated throughout the whole world, the apostolic lord, Zacharias'. But it was in connection with the setting up of a third metropolitan see at Lichfield that papal action was directly invoked. Pope Gregory had established the two provinces of the English Church and only the papacy could set his arrangements aside by the erection of a third metropolitan see; in the end, it was the massive objection of the English clergy to changing the Gregorian scheme that led to the failure of the plan for a third province.

The Mercian scheme for the advancement of the see of Lichfield was political rather than apostolic: not the desire for more bishops to convert the heathen, but for the counsellor bishop of the strongest of the English kings at the time to be honoured as metropolitan. The use of the old title of *bretwalda* had died with the Northumbrian kings, Oswald and Oswiu; after their day the commanding position, though not the title, passed to the kings of Mercia. King Æthelbald, who ruled from 716 till 757, was a warrior king, who had some kind of political supremacy over the kings south of the Humber and ruled London in the south of his own kingdom. It was he who was present at, and probably presided over, the reforming council of Clofeshoh, 746, but he was personally a rough and violent ruler with no great interest in learning or church reform. He was succeeded, however, by King Offa, who was much more than a warrior king. He maintained a learned court, he corresponded with Charlemagne, he invaded and crushed the kingdom of Kent, and he desired that the see of Lichfield should be at least the equal of Canterbury.

Offa impressed that wise and far-seeing statesman, Pope Hadrian I, as a ruler to be conciliated and if possible used in the interests of the Church. The English Church had acknowledged its spiritual parentage in 746: but no direct embassy had ever been sent from Rome since the days of Augustine. Pope Hadrian in 787 now sent two legates to England, to the court of King Offa, hoping both to promote the reform of the Church by synod, and to enter into friendly relations with King Offa. The legates were received by Archbishop Jænberht at Canterbury 'where the body of St Augustine' rests: Jænberht, whose lands had been largely seized by the conquering Offa, and whose episcopal mint, the mint at Canterbury, was now being used for the minting of Offa's coins. The legates wrote to Pope Hadrian, reporting that Jænberht had received their admonishment, without mention of any joyful welcome; but Offa the king received them in his hall with very great joy.

The legates, taking counsel with the English kings Offa and Cynewulf of Wessex, together with the bishops, agreed and subscribed a long list of ecclesiastical reforms, and though the erection of the metropolitan see of Mercia does not appear in the legatine acts, the see was actually set up, and the pallium was sent to the first archbishop, Hygeberht, in the year following (788). After the southern synod, in 787, one of the legates travelled north, and a northern synod was held under the legate, Archbishop Eanbald of York and his bishops and the king of Northumbria. Many things, the legates wrote, needed correction: 'for, as you know, from the time of Augustine no Roman bishop has been sent here, except ourselves'.

The erection of the Lichfield see at the expense of Canterbury, by subtracting certain dioceses from the southern province, had however only been made possible by the political dominance of Offa. Kent and the church of Canterbury continued bitterly resentful. When Offa died, in 796, revolt at once broke out in the under kingdoms of Kent and Wessex; King Cenwulf of Mercia was in a much less strong position than Offa. He wrote to Pope Leo III, quoting the text of Pope Gregory's letter about the two provinces: a letter well known to the Mercian clergy through Bede's history. He suggested that Gregory had actually authorised the setting up of the southern metropolitan see at London, not Canterbury, and his enactment had never been carried out. To have the see transferred from Canterbury to London would have suited the king of Mercia very well: it appeared a compromise, for the Lichfield plan was dropped, and it appeared strictly canonical, as following exactly Pope Gregory's letter. But it called for the setting aside of two centuries of English history; it did not settle the Kentish-Mercian quarrel or restore the lands taken by Offa from the see of Canterbury; and, above all, it did not reckon with the reverence of the Mercian clergy themselves for the see of Canterbury. It was too widely known that Augustine sleeps at Canterbury.

In 803 Archbishop Æthelheard of Canterbury convened a synod at Clofeshoh, and announced that Pope Hadrian's grant to Offa of the metropolis at Lichfield had been obtained by misrepresentation, and was therefore null and void. Archbishop Hygeberht himself had resigned before the council, and his successors at Lichfield did not claim metropolitan rank.

## CHAPTER 8

# The *Vita Monachica* in England after Augustine

No summary of Augustine's work in England, and the fruit of that work, would be complete without some reference to the English minsters and the *vita monachica* lived there. There were as yet no Benedictine monks, and no canons; the centuries between Augustine and Charlemagne were the centuries of the 'mixed rule', in England as elsewhere in western Europe. Men lived in the monasteries, the minsters (two forms of the same word), as monks, under obedience to an abbot, saying the *opus dei*, engaged in various works within the monastery and, as far as the abbot himself was concerned, having some pastoral obligations to the people of the countryside. Whether the minster were Celtic or founded in the Mediterranean tradition, the monks looked back to Egypt and the holiness of the desert Fathers. The Celts were clerks and not governed by the ideal of stability within one monastery: a Celtic abbot expected to make pastoral journeys, attended by a few monks. Monks in the Canterbury tradition looked back to the house monastery of the Rule of the Master and St Benedict: they were not clerks, except as chosen by the abbot for training for the priesthood: the people would come to their church for the great festivals, or for baptism, and, gradually, the abbots established churches on their more distant lands, that the people should not have to come so far. Some of the very earliest rural parishes[1] were thus founded. The bishops too founded churches on their estates; kings travelled round with their chaplains, and attended on the great feasts the see churches in their capitals, where the bishop and his *familia* of clergy had their home and headquarters. Sooner or later, the thegns too built themselves private churches near their halls, and the villagers attended. But in the centuries immediately following Augustine, it was those who led the *vita monachica* within the minsters who counted for most in the

---

[1] See Deanesly, *Pre-Conquest Church*, p. 197, and the whole of chap. ix, 'Minster and parish'

service of the English Church, and also of the king (apart from fighting).

In the seventh century, the time of the gradual conversion of the whole of England, not only the monks, but the bishop and his clergy were said to live in a minster. Christ Church at Canterbury was a minster, perhaps naturally, since Augustine had brought his monks there; Egbert lived in the minster at York, Eata at Hexham, Wilfrid at Ripon, bishops Haeddi and Daniel in the Old Minster at Winchester. To the townsmen every enclosure for holy men was a minster, for those inside were all dedicated to God's service. They had the tonsure, they had no wives, and they lived communally, whether they were the bishop's clergy or the 'serfs of God' living under an abbot.

But pastoral work was not the monks' or the clergy's sole service to the king, who gave such large endowments to minsters, whether of bishops or abbots. The minsters were schools and 'universities': there were no others. This does not mean that they afforded any general education for the people at large, for no such thing was thought of; apart from the upper classes, eorls and thegns, who might or might not learn to read English writing, the ceorls and the læts and the varying social classes learned their farm-work and ploughing, their smith-craft and weaving and dyeing, the way to snare birds and catch fish, traditionally, as they grew up. They knew the penalties for offences, the dooms of the folk moot. They knew the old folk tales, the long songs the *scopas* sang at the king's feast, or that they themselves sang when the cup was passed round at the ale house. But they did not learn to read and write. That was the special craft of priests and monks.

It was in the minsters that study, much as that described in detail in the old Rule of the Master, went on, for this old rule was an exceptionally long description of the *vita monachica* as widely known and practised. Minsters were endowed by kings in regions still pagan and no doubt as a focus of evangelisation: but the practice of the *vita monachica* within them, the education of youths and boys for the service of God, was primary, and pastoral work incidental. In the minsters children were trained, at a set time in the day, to read in the 'larger alphabets', and those with promise were promoted to rubbing down with pumice the vellum sheets as they came from the tanner, to making the ink, ruling the lines upon the page, and copying the text of one manuscript on to another. The writing of choir books and books of the scriptures was the first necessity for the minster; but the abbot or *praepositus* always desired to have other books for the book chest. Books were brought from Italy or Gaul for the minsters, sometimes as gifts, often as purchased by the abbot or his messenger. Books were borrowed from other minsters and copied before return. Whether the minster were a bishop's minster, where he educated his young clergy, or an abbot's minster, where he trained his young brothers in the *vita monachica*, books and learning were important.

The Kentish minsters[1] were a group founded early, and mainly by the kings of Kent on their royal estates, beside the old Roman roads: there were at first no other churches than those of the minsters. The Watling Street, which was a Roman road before it gained its Saxon name from the Watlinga, a tribe living to the north-west of Londinium, ran from the Channel ports to Londinium, and then on to the north-west. In Kent the old roads ran from Dover and Folkestone, joined, and went on to the ford at Durovernum: minsters were founded at both ports, on the king's estates. That at Folkestone was founded, *c.* 640, for Eanswythe, the king's daughter: in the late legend of her life, she needed water and commanded the river to run uphill to her minster, and it did. The old road ran through Durovernum, and here the king gave land for Augustine's see church and his monastery. Then it ran westward to Rochester, where Æthelberht made a bishop's minster, and north-westward to Londinium; between Rochester and the Thames bank was built later the minster of Hogh or Hoo.

Two other minsters between the Watling Street and Thames bank were called locally simply 'the minster': Minster in Sheppey and Minster in Thanet. Queen Seaxburg, wife of King Earconberht of Kent, founded the minster in Sheppey after her husband died in the plague of 664; she had come from East Anglia herself, and chose a site where a road, branching north from the Watling Street, crossed the island of Sheppey and continued by way of a ferry across Thames mouth. A princess minster like this one on Sheppey had a good staff of chaplains for the nuns, and to them the people of the country-

[1] See *ibid.*, pp. 202–6

side came for baptism and teaching. Minster in Thanet was also
a princess minster. The great minster of Lyminge, founded for
Æthelburga and Paulinus has been mentioned earlier; that of
Reculver (Raculf) was founded by King Egbert for Bassa, his
mass priest. In all these Kentish minsters the abbot or abbess
ruled, mapping out the daily hours of office and work, the daily
custom, according to their own training or such monastic rules
as might have reached them, in the Mediterranean tradition.

This monastic tradition reached northern England when
Medehamstede was founded, and when Benedict Biscop
founded Monkwearmouth and Jarrow, and Bishop Wilfrid
founded his minsters of Ripon and Hexham. Eddius, Wilfrid's
biographer, tells how Wilfrid, arguing against his opponents at
the synod of Aetswinapath (?703), claimed that he had been
forty years a bishop and had changed and converted the whole
of Northumbria from the Celtic practice: 'And did I not
arrange the life of the monks in accordance with the rule of the
holy father Benedict which none had previously introduced
there?' Which was no doubt true of Northumbria, and, as
implying an exclusive following of the Benedictine rule, true
probably of the whole of Britain. But the statement by no means
excludes knowledge of the Benedictine rule by Benedict Biscop,
among the eighteen monastic rules he collected, and as his
name suggests; nor does it exclude knowledge of the Benedictine rule much earlier by Gregory and Augustine and the
minsters of Kent.

An early minster that, with its daughter houses, must have
done much for the conversion of the midland districts, was that
of Medehamstede. It cannot be proved to have been founded
either in the Mediterranean tradition, or in that of the Celts,
though its dedication points to inspiration from Canterbury
*via* East Anglia. It was to be the great non-episcopal monastery
of the Mercians. Bede does not mention its foundation directly,
but he says that when Archbishop Theodore deprived Wynfrith
of his bishopric of the Mercians (in 675), he ordained in his
place Seaxwulf, who was the abbot and builder of the monastery
of Medehamstede.

The Anglo-Saxon Chronicle, put together by King Alfred's
scribes in the south of England, had no mention of Medehamstede in its earliest versions. But the so-called Laud version of

the Chronicle was compiled, almost certainly, at York and has certain additions concerned with northern affairs, derived from sources accessible in the early tenth century at York. One of these northern additions to the Wessex Chronicle is an account of the foundation of Medehamstede. It relates how Penda and thirty princes with him were slain at the battle of the Winwood:

> And Peada, son of Penda, succeeded to the kingdom of Mercia. In his time they came together, he and Oswiu, brother of King Oswald, and declared that they wished to establish a monastery to the glory of Christ and to the honour of St Peter. And they so did, and gave it the name Medehamstede, because there is a spring there called Medeswæl. . . . And they entrusted it to a monk who was called Seaxwulf. He was a great friend of God, and all people loved him, and he was very nobly born in the world and powerful. He is now much more powerful with Christ.

But King Peada did not reign for long: he was killed in the year 656, and his brother Wulfhere reigned in his stead. But the king loved Medehamstede, for the love of his brother Peada, and for love of his sworn brother, Oswiu, and for love of Seaxwulf its abbot.

> Then sent the king for the abbot to come quickly to him and he did so. Then spake the king to the abbot, 'O beloved Seaxwulf . . . my brother Peada and my dear friend Oswiu began a monastery to the glory of God and of St Peter, but my brother, as Christ willed it, has departed this life; but I wish to ask you, O beloved friend, to have the men labour quickly at the work, and I will find you gold and silver and land and property and all that is needed for it.' The abbot went home and began to work . . . so that in a few years the monastery was finished.

The king hearing this was very glad, and sent for the archbishop, bishops, eorls, thegns, and all those who loved God to come to him for the consecration of the monastery. And there were present with him at the consecration his brother Æthelred and his sisters Cyneburh and Cyneswith, and Archbishop Deusdedit consecrated the monastery, and there were also present Ithamar, bishop of Rochester, and the bishop of London called Wine, and the bishop of the Mercians called Jaruman, and Bishop Tuda; and the priest Wilfrid, who was afterwards a bishop. And King Wulfhere gave to Abbot

Seaxwulf and his monks and to St Peter all the lands and waters and meres and fens and (fish) weirs. Then followed in the Chronicle the line of the boundary of the abbey lands, as it ran through the places named. And the abbot said that he had here God-fearing monks who would like to spend their lives in an anchorite's cell, if they knew where; and here in the fens and meres given to him he found an island, where their monastery should stand. And the monastery so flourished that it sent out daughter houses to Breedon on the Hill, in Leicestershire, to Brixworth, where the lovely Saxon church still stands, to Bermondsey and to Woking; apparently also, to Hogh or Hoo, near the road on which a Mercian abbot or king would travel, if he wished to cross Thames mouth, on his way to Canterbury.

Medehamstede then, so early founded, before ever the synod of Whitby was held or Archbishop Theodore selected by the pope for the see of Canterbury, was typically a monastery of the 'mixed rule'. Under Seaxwulf, as in Augustine's monastery at Canterbury, men lived the *vita monachica*, and there is no need to ask which written rule they followed, for they lived under the rule of their abbot. A flexible rule, this, and able to combine pastoral work with work in the monastery, at the abbot's discretion. A rule whose very flexibility made it, in the long run, dangerous; as is shown even in the pages of Bede. But a rule that could produce the learning and statesmanship of Abbot Hadrian of Canterbury, the sanctity of a Cuthbert at Lindisfarne, or an Æthelthryd at Ely.

Augustine sleeps at Canterbury, and in the long centuries before the Norman Conquest Englishmen never forgot it. Of all the things he did, after his baptism of the king and the men of Kent, perhaps the most enduring and notable were the setting up of the English hierarchy in two provinces to consecrate and rule the English clergy, and the introduction of the old *vita monachica* according to the tradition of the Mediterranean.

# Appendix 1

## The Rule of the Master (RM) and the
## Rule of St Benedict (RSB)

THE Rule of the Master and the Rule of St Benedict were both conceived of as a recording of the far older tradition of the monastic life. In many monasteries the abbot arranged his own monastic timetable, summoning the monks by signal to the hours of the divine office as they punctuated the day, but without writing down the rule of the monastery as regards timetable or discipline.

We have, however, certain historical references to abbots who did write down a rule, as well as to some famous monasteries where the rule was not written. Lérins was a house famous for its observance, but we know of no rule as written by its founder, Honoratus. We hear that Abbot John of Réomé (d. 539) ruled his own monastery first by tradition and without written rule, and that he retired from the monastery and was recalled by his bishop. To fulfil his charge more perfectly, he then went to Lérins and stayed there unrecognised for eighteen months to learn the observance of the house, which he then took back to Réomé as the 'rule of St Makarios' (the desert Father: see for his association with the Rule of the Master, p. 137). Similarly Lubin, who founded a monastery at Brou, had studied the observance of Lérins.

There were, however, in the sixth century, monasteries where a written rule was followed. Bishop Caesarius of Arles (d. 543) wrote a *Regula ad virgines*, and Bishop Aurelian of Arles (d. 551) wrote rules for monks and nuns respectively. Bishop Augustine of Hippo (d. 430) had lived monastically, communally, with his clergy, as was described by his friend and biographer, Possidius, and he had written a rule for nuns which has survived in his Letter 211. It has been assumed that this rule was substantially the same as the rule which he and his clergy followed and was, in the contemporary sense, a monastic rule; its primary text was the apostolic record, 'No man said that he had anything of his own, but they had all things in common.' Evidence that some

sixth-century abbots wrote rules to enshrine their own observance is supported by the statement that Aredius (d. 591)
founded a monastery at Attane, where the rules of Cassian,
Basil and 'the other abbots' was followed. Cassiodorus founded
his monastery of Vivarium (Squillace), on the Adriatic coast,
soon after his return from Constantinople, about A.D. 548; there
is no direct evidence about the rule which his monastery followed, but surviving manuscripts show that an early version of
the old RM was known and copied at Vivarium.

There is plenty of evidence, then, that in the century of
St Benedict, Pope Gregory and Augustine, there was a well-
understood tradition of the monastic life, and that some abbots
ruled their monasteries by this tradition, consulting at will such
written rules as were accessible to them. For all the monasteries
the tradition that service of God in the manner of Christ's withdrawal to the wilderness was regarded as central; but to such
service an urgent need to exercise Christian compassion might
add the succouring of travellers or the sick, or, in the east,
orphans or pilgrims. The copying of manuscripts was needed
for the welfare of the monastery itself; the child oblates must be
taught their letters, as all monks should be unless they were of
advanced age; psalters must be written and books of the
scriptures for the Lessons of the night office and for study,
altar books of the gospels, and commentaries and treatises on
theology by the catholic Fathers. The life of the monk was in no
way pastoral: but, if pagans surrounded the monastery and
came for instruction, it was as much an alms to teach them the
faith as to feed their bodies with bread.

The circumstances of the writing down of the RSB are well
known from the account of St Benedict's life, work and miracles
given by Pope Gregory in his book called the *Dialogues,* but
nothing is certainly known of the writing down of the RM, and
controversy has arisen about the relationship of the one to the
other. Which was written first? and in which rule, if either, was
Augustine trained? Or, is such a question inconsistent with the
historical setting, since all abbots of the greater monasteries
studied such rules as were accessible to them and no abbot
accepted any of them without modification, even if he did not
write down his own particular observance?

Augustine in the monastery *ad clivum Scauri,* the well-endowed monastery of an eminent and living founder, would have been trained by an abbot instructed in monastic rules. It is difficult to imagine that, among them, he would not have had at hand some form of the long and detailed RM, with all its scriptural quotations to buttress its prescriptions, and the much shorter, but profound and paternal, provisions of the RSB.

Controversy about the relationship of the RM and the RSB has hinged upon the fact that many phrases, and two long sections, are common to both. It used to be believed that the RM was a later commentary on the RSB but modern scholarship has now accepted that the longer rule was the older. It is, in fact, accepted, that the RM, in an early form, was known to Cassiodorus and was copied in his monastery of Vivarium, and was also known to St Benedict at Monte Cassino. Benedict, in writing his own rule, which was necessary partly because the RM was so exceedingly long, and partly because the old, classical rules were too imprecise for the guidance of his own monastery, and too old-fashioned, copied or had copied for his own rule passages from the RM which seemed to him terse and sufficient: as, for instance, the chapter on the four kinds of monks, and a long passage on 'the kind of man an abbot ought to be'. His rule, however, was not a mere condensation and précis of the RM, and it was not merely more modern in liturgical directions, more suited to a sixth-century Italian monk because one stage further removed from the régime of the desert Fathers than the RM: in the RSB the relation of the abbot to the community showed some modification. The RSB, shaping monastic practice in a monastery threatened by the new invaders of Europe, was, in fact, to become later a factor in the new civilisation; the RM looked back to Egypt and the past.

The authorship of the RM is unknown: its original title was simply the *Regula Patrum* or *Regula Sanctorum Patrum*, meaning the desert Fathers, an indistinctive title when all monasteries aimed at following the monastic tradition of the desert. The treatise is in the form of a dialogue between a *Magister* and a *Discipulus*, and it was only when Benedict of Aniane first incorporated it in his *Concordia Regularum* that he called it the 'Rule of the Master'. No one knows for what monastery it was, in its earliest form, intended. It was a description of the monastic, coenobitic life, the contemplative life. This consisted essentially in a complete renunciation of life in the world and of self direction: the new brother entered the monastery and promised to lead the life of heavenly conversation; the Latin phrase, *conversatio morum meorum*, was epexegetic, or doubly emphatic, like *proelia certaminum*. The new life thus entered upon was founded on the teaching of four great Egyptian ascetics. The prologue opens with: 'Here begins the rule of the holy fathers, Serapion, Makarios, Panuthios and the other Makarios', and goes on to state that 'As we sat in one council, established as most healthful, we asked the Lord our God to grant us the Holy Spirit to instruct us how we should ordain a rule for this [monastic] life. Serapion said that since the earth is full of the mercy of the Lord and many bands are striving towards the summit of the blessed life, it seems best of all to obey the commands of the Holy Spirit. We cannot establish words which are ours alone, except the sure foundation of the scripture affirms our ordinance. For the Holy Spirit saith: "Behold how good and joyful a thing it is, brethren, to dwell together in unity". And again: "He maketh men to be of one mind in a house". . . . The purpose of this rule, confirmed by the Holy Spirit' the prologue continues, 'is to enable men to dwell together in joyful unanimity. We will that one man be head of this holy congregation. The scriptures say: "Obey them that have the rule over you: Obey those set over you [*praepositis vestris*]", and again: "I will have obedience and not sacrifice".'

After many pages of the teaching of Serapion, Makarios speaks, and then Panuthios and the other Makarios. Then follows the *Thema*, a discourse on the Lord's Prayer, and then the ninety-five chapters of the rule. Chapter I deals with the four kinds of monks, Chapter II with what kind of man an abbot ought to be, and both were mainly incorporated in the RSB later. The opening sentence of the chapter dealing with obedience (Chapter VII) is the same as that in St Benedict's discourse on humility: 'The first step (*grade*) in humility is obedience without delay.' The aphorism must have been widely known in the monastic tradition.

It is in keeping with the exalted and mystical position given to the abbot in the RM, that no single officer is given the position of second-in-command; it accords with the natural grouping of bands of monks around an ascetic famed for his holiness back in the Thebaid, an abbot or father whose holiness is his only title to authority. The eleventh chapter of the RM is headed: About the '*praepositi* of the monastery', and states that 'the *praepositi* shall be so ordered as to have charge each of ten brothers'. The abbot shall ordain the greater (*maiores*: for senior) members of the family, whom the lesser members shall fear as representing the lord (*vice domini*). These senior monks are not spoken of as deans (*decani*), but elsewhere they are spoken of as each having a decade of monks. The RM here explains that not only are its precepts confirmed by Scripture but that the organisation of the monasteries parallels that of the bishop and his *familia* in the see. 'In the Church God has ordained bishops, priests, deacons and clergy, whose commands, given in God's name, the plebs hear and obey.' Similarly, in the monasteries there are abbots and *praepositi*, whom, for their souls' sakes, the monks shall hear and obey. 'In monasteries as in the Church God saith: "He that heareth you, heareth me".' Later in the RM, it is laid down that the abbot shall publicly institue the senior by giving him the rod of office (*virga*).

The liturgical directions in the RM, the *Ordo Officii*, occupy Chapters XXXIII to XLVI and do not correspond with those of the RSB: they witness to a less-developed state of the liturgy. The evening office which St Benedict calls vespers is spoken of by the earlier name as the *lucernaria*. No certainty of the anteriority of the RM follows from this, however, for there was, as yet, no unification of the liturgy: an old-fashioned office might be said in one place and a more developed form in another. Nevertheless, the liturgical evidence tends to confirm other and more positive signs of anteriority.

Wherever the RM was written, it was, in fact, written in Latin and envisaged the monks as living in a typical Greco-Roman villa house. They sleep in a large hall or banqueting room, an *atrium* or *triclinium*; their monastery is not a *laura*, with the huts of the monks clustered round that of the holy anchorite to whom they have attached themselves. This material Latin setting is combined with an atmosphere of Egyptian holiness, for, as mentioned above, the abbot in the RM rules by virtue of grace granted him directly by God, i.e. charismatic grace. It was not a grace conferred on him by the ecclesiastical hierarchy: the monk's obedience to him was obedience given directly to the Holy Spirit, and to Christ. In conformity with this atmosphere, there was no council to help the abbot in major decisions (as there was to be in the RSB).

Both day and night for the monk following the RM were to be broken up by the canonical hours, recited in the oratory. When the signal for a divine hour has struck in the oratory, immediately those working put down their work, the craftsmen lay aside their tools, the scribes leave unfinished the letter they had begun to write and all the brethren take their hands from what they were doing. They at once proceed gravely to the oratory. The brethren on a journey take with them a little book (*codicillum*) with the Lessons for the office they are missing (the psalms they will know by heart). The night office in the RM is called matins, and the day offices are spoken of as 'the day hours of canonical praises, seven in number'.

There is much in the RM about the child oblates and their instruction, and something about the education of older monks. 'From prime till terce,' the RM enjoins, 'each decade is at work, and they have leisure to read. The children in these three hours study in their decade on their parchment tables (*tabulae*), instructed by a lettered monk.' They shall learn 'the greater alphabets' up to the age of fifty; 'let those that cannot read learn the psalms by heart, all in their respective decades. The *praepositi* are to collect the parchment tables and the books when it is time for terce.' Which meant, apparently, that all children and monks up to the age of fifty must be able to read the capital letters of Roman inscriptions, which, as written with a pen, would be what palaeographers call 'uncials'. When the RM was drawn up, the more rapidly written cursive letters were not yet in common use: psalters and service books would then and for long afterwards be written in uncials.

'After terce, the *praepositi* inquire from the abbot where their decade is to work, at work of different kinds. They shall work always in silence. Then they go to sext. A lettered monk shall be appointed to read to those at work: he shall be one whom, through some impossibility of nature, the abbot cannot set to work himself.'

The rule also gives directions about the monks' siesta and sleep at nights. Chapter XXVIII is headed: 'About their sleeping time and where they shall sleep and in what manner. In summer-time, when sext has been said, either on a fast day or when they have eaten, all shall rest, so that even when (summer) nights are short the brethren shall rise soberly and swiftly from sleep for the divine office (*opus divinum*) and prayer. For in one *atrium* or *triclinium* the beds shall be arranged in order in a circle, and in the midst of the circle the abbot shall have his bed, so that he may watch over the silence and reverence of the circle, and like a careful shepherd keep watch over his whole flock of sheep now collected in one sheepfold.'

In view of the lack of documentary or external evidence of the writing of the RM, and its evident relationship of some sort with the RSB, the anteriority of the RM rests on a comparison of the words used in the text. Of 75 words investigated by philologists, 53 occur only in the first seven chapters of the RSB, the part it has largely in common with the RM, while they continue to be employed regularly throughout the whole of the RM. St Benedict, that is, borrowed them when borrowing largely from the RM, but did not use them in the chapters he was writing, or dictating, independently. Moreover, the word *autem*, which occurs 78 times in the independent chapters of the RSB (VIII to LXXIII), is not known in the RM; it is St Benedict's word.

The question of the authorship of the RM remains open. The authorship of Cassiodorus has been asserted and much debated, but not however accepted. Cassiodorus was a great and learned statesman and a man of wealth; he served under the Gothic kings in the north of Italy and sought to pass on to the Goths the Italian heritage of Roman law, administration and learning. In 540, however, the general of the East Roman emperor took Ravenna, the Gothic capital, and Cassiodorus, the chief Gothic minister, was allowed to retire from public life. After some years, and probably soon after his return from a voyage to Constantinople in 548, he founded a monastery on his paternal estate at Squillace on the Adriatic. He was the most learned man in Italy and had abundant resources; his monastery from the beginning would seem to have been large. It was, however, at some time wrecked by the invading Lombards and its beautifully written manuscripts were dispersed; two manuscripts of the RM, which the editors of the RM regard as having been written about 600, have survived. These cannot have been the manuscripts of the RM used by St Benedict at Monte Cassino, for he died about 548, before the time of the foundation of Vivarium. But he and the scribes at Vivarium must have used an earlier manuscript, and perhaps an earlier edition, of the RM, earlier than the manuscripts copied by the scribes of the two oldest extant manuscripts. Critics who examined the RM, comparing it with Cassiodorus's works, to determine if possible whether Cassiodorus himself wrote the RM, found evidence from Cassiodurus's *Commentary on the Psalms* that he knew the RM rather than that he wrote it. This agrees with the fact that St Benedict was using the RM before his death, some years before the foundation of Vivarium.

The authorship of the RM has also been sought at Lérins, and the theory supported by the reference to Abbot Réomé as having brought from Lérins and practised in his own house 'the rule of Makarios'. It is not, however, possible that any 'rule of Makarios' should have been actually written by either saint of that name so as to become the prototype of the RM, for both the fourth-century abbots of this name lived before any community with a complete day and night timetable was established. Nor was the monastery of Honoratus at Lérins a house monastery: expert specialist opinion in France is against it, nor have remains of any Roman villa been discovered on the islands. The original monastery must have been of the *laura type*, with a group of cells, but no *atrium*.

The reference to Makarios, however, is an indication of the general reverence in which the Egyptian monks were held, and is of interest in connection with the prologue of the RM, and the extent to which sixth-century western monks were familiar with the *Lausiac History* of Palladius, as well as other authorities on Egyptian monastic life. Of the two abbots Makarios, one is found termed 'the elder', 'the Egyptian', and 'the ancient', the other 'the younger' and 'the Alexandrian'. Both are mentioned in the *Paradisus Heraclidis* as well as in the *Lausiac History*. Both lived in the Egyptian deserts in the fourth century, the one in the region known as Scete, the other in that of the cells (*cellae*) of the Thebaid. Both were made priests for the benefit of the many solitaries who settled around them.

To neither hermit do early sources attribute the writing of

any rule, though to Makarios of Egypt certain *Apothegmata* are attributed, and to both many short homilies and exhortations. The holiness of both hermits is attested by their asceticism, corporal austerities and the miracles they performed; much more space is allotted to those of the younger Makarios, as better known, in the *Lausiac History*. Of the latter, it is stated that he sought admission to the monastery of Pachomius in Tabennisi as an old man, and was refused entrance by the abbot on the ground that he could not, at his age, endure the austerities of monks who had entered as young men. The prolonged silence and fasting of Makarios in Lent, however, astonished the *praepositus* of the monastery, one of the many under the guidance of Pachomius, and he prayed, and it was revealed to him that this was indeed Makarios, the priest and hermit of whose holiness he had long heard; Makarios was then welcomed to become a monk of the monastery. None of the chapters in which Palladius records the life and miracles of this Makarios makes any mention of a rule composed by him: and, indeed, the description of the *vita monachica* in his time and that of the elder Makarios precludes the drawing up of a rule where a common night and day timetable should be followed by a community of monks.

Thus no 'rule of Makarios' followed at Lérins could have been prescribed by either Makarios, though it is understandable that the abbot of a house monastery should have represented the rule he drew up as the salutary advice of the blessed abbots Makarios the Elder and the Younger, of Panuthios the pupil of Makarios the Younger, and of Hilarion.

Pope Gregory, our only primary source for the life and work of St Benedict, has nothing to say about the RM. It does not follow from this that he was unacquainted with it or that the abbot who trained him *ad clivum Scauri* was unacquainted with it. Gregory would have held it to be, as its *explicit* asserts, the *Regula Sanctorum Patrum*: but then, all monastic rules, written or unwritten, were crystallisations of the 'Rule of the holy [Egyptian] Fathers'. Gregory in the *Dialogues* was dealing with the miracles of holy men of his own age, and he knew neither the author of the RM, nor any miracles vouchsafed to attest his holiness.

He knew of many, however, to attest the holiness of St

Benedict, and for that reason if for no others he devoted to him the whole of Book II of his *Dialogues*. He wrote the treatise as a dialogue with his younger friend, the papal deacon Peter. There is no evidence that Peter had ever been a monk before he passed into the papal service: but the contemporary interest in monasticism of the papal *familia* at the Vatican is well attested. Pope Gregory expressly mentions St Benedict's writing of a rule in the *Dialogues*:

> It would be pleasant, Peter, now to narrate many other matters concerning the venerable father, but certain deeds of his I intentionally omit, because I am hastening in due course to his other deeds. But this I will not conceal from you, that the man of God, among the many miracles for which he was famous in the world, shone in no normal manner by word of doctrine. For he wrote a rule for monks outstanding in discretion and beautifully worded. And if any man will study his life and manners with more subtlety, he may find in the rule thus instituted all the acts of his teaching (*magisterii*). For the holy man could not teach otherwise than as he lived.

From the account in the *Dialogues* and from certain of Pope Gregory's letters, it is clear that Benedict intended his rule only for his monks at Monte Cassino. He did not expect even the daughter monastery of Terracina to keep the rule exclusively, though the monks sent there had apparently been trained in his own rule. For instance: he himself preferred, and (following the RM) directed, that a monastery, if large, should be ruled under the abbot by seniors called deans (*decani*), not by a single senior called a *praepositus*; yet he sent the colony of monks to Terracina under the leadership of a single *praepositus*. Such an arrangement would supply the single authority on the spot needed in a new foundation.

The fact that Benedict states in the RSB that other abbots may, if they wish, copy his arrangement of psalms and canticles in the divine office, does not imply that they had any direct relationship with himself: there was no 'Benedictine order'. According to contemporary usage, Benedict implies that other abbots may wish to copy his arrangements, or vary them at will, as he himself was free to borrow from older rules. He mentioned the arrangement of psalms as material that other abbots might wish to borrow, and possibly because, as modern scholars have shown, he was here keeping very close to the arrangements of the office in the Roman basilicas (see p. 155): these might be less familiar to other abbots without his early Roman background, or associations. In short, Benedict represents his own rule, in the text of the RSB, as a careful redaction of his knowledge of the monastic tradition; he speaks of it as *regula sancta, magistra regula,* for that reason. Other abbots may choose to follow that tradition as he has written it down; they and their monks who wish to pass to greater heights of holiness should study the rules of those giants of the past, Pachomius, Cassian and Basil.

It has been asked, indeed, whether Benedict, in drawing up his rule, was making more than a compilation. Bishops who composed canons for councils, lawyers who composed codes for the emperor, abbot-bishops who composed penitentials, all used older material and without acknowledgment. The so-called Breviary of Alaric, issued as a code for the Visigoths by Alaric II, a code for his Roman subjects in Gaul and Spain, was just a compilation.

Benedict's work, however, was different. It is true that he was writing, in a sense, a code of law: a monastic code. The Latin word *regula* in his day was interchangeable with the Greek *kanon,* for the translators of Justinian's Latin Code into Greek put *kanon* where they found *regula* in the original. Benedict was writing a code of law for his monks of Monte Cassino, and the incorporation of older material gave weight to a new code. Yet Benedict's work was not merely a compilation. It was an individual effort, to provide 'a little rule for beginners', the 'rule of a beginning'.

Benedict in writing the RSB, that is, was not just meeting the difficulty that the RM was so long that its mere length (in the opinion of modern editors) prevented its copying and diffusion. He was not just copying in succession relevant passages from Cassian, Basil and the Code of Justinian. He was not legislating for large bodies of monks, as the bishops in council drew up canons to be observed by large bodies of the faithful, large numbers of the clergy, or even a number of monasteries. He was writing down an individual rule for his own monastery, his own monks, and for no others. He was not writing a general treatise on the monastic life, wherein holy admonition and discourse on the degrees of asceticism, or of contemplative prayer, flowed from his pen, like the *Verba Seniorum* of the Egyptian anchorites. He was responsible for the souls of his monks, and for them only: he must order their daily life so that all of them, the weak as well as the strong, might lead the *vita monachica* and obey in their abbot Christ himself. Benedict again and again echoed Cassian: but their rules had a century of monastic practice between them.

The RM, as far as explicit identification by any title goes, was unmentioned by either St Benedict or Pope Gregory; but then, it had at the time no specific title nor was it attributed to a named author. Benedict's quotation of long passages from it shows that he at any rate was familiar with it. He mentions specifically the rules of Basil and Cassian and if he had known the writer of the RM he might have included him with them: as it was, he probably held the RM as one form, a good and holy form, of the traditional *Regula Sanctorum Patrum*. The RM, along with the rules of Basil and Cassian, probably played its part in the training of Augustine in his Roman monastery, as they did in Benedict's monastery at Monte Cassino. Benedict had a great reverence for the old rules, as demanding greater strictness, a longer burden of office, and as it were greater holiness than he was himself prepared to ask of all his own monks. He wrote, as he tells us himself in the RSB, 'a little rule for beginners' in the monastic life—what his contemporaries would have thought of as a rule for modern monks, not merely a recapitulation of the requirements of those giants of the past, Makarios, Panuthios, Serapion, Pachomius, Cassian and Basil. In the last chapter of the RSB he wrote:

Now we have written out this rule in order that by observing it in our monasteries we may show ourselves to have, to some degree, integrity of life, or the beginning at least of conversion [*conversatio morum*]. For the rest, for those who hasten to the perfection of conversion, there are the teachings of the holy fathers, whose observance brings a man to the height of perfection: and indeed what page or what discourse of the divine authority of the Old and New Testament is not a most unerring pattern of human life? Or what book of the holy Catholic fathers does not ringingly proclaim, how by a straight course we may come to our Creator?

Moreover, the *Collations* of the fathers [Cassian's], the *Institutes* [Cassian's] and their Lives, yes and the rule of our holy father, St Basil, what else are these but instruments of virtue in the hands of good-living and obedient monks? But to us, indolent and ill-living and negligent, they bring the red blush of confusion. Whosoever thou art, therefore, who hastenest to the heavenly country, fulfil, Christ helping thee, this very little rule of a beginning.

St Benedict echoes Cassian's phrases here and often elsewhere in his rule: as in 'the beginning of conversion', 'those who haste to the perfection of conversion', 'the lofty heights of perfection'. The custom of acknowledging verbal borrowings, and even the incorporation of long passages, was still far in the future.

Benedict looked back not only to Cassian but behind him to the monks of Egypt as the exemplars of the monastic life. Cassian's *Collations* recounted the teaching of the desert Fathers in the form of interviews given to inquirers: Cassian himself had travelled to the distant desert of the Thebaid in 385, and remained there seven years, visiting the different cells. In the *Collations* he recounted the interior and exterior *ascesis* of the Fathers (Makarios, Pambo, Bessarion, etc.), and he knew their efforts to attain *apatheia*, the 'not-being-disturbed' by any outward thing. In his *Institutes* he recounted 'observances of the outer man', the daily life, clothes, customs and observances of these same monks.

He would have known the collection of anecdotes about them, of their sayings, that were being bandied about in Coptic, Greek and Syriac, and were found mainly as Greek collections, known as the *apothegmata patrum*, and in Latin translations as the *Verba Seniorum*. They came to be joined in manuscript to the other collection about the desert Fathers, the *Vitae Patrum*, which St Benedict mentions; St Jerome translated a series of these biographies, of Paul the first hermit, Hilarion, Malchus, etc., and Rufinus of Aquileia another series which he called *Historia Monachorum*.

Greek monks, like St Basil, also visited the Egyptian desert, founded monasteries round the east Mediterranean and in Constantinople, and made Greek collections of the desert Fathers' lives and sayings. Latin translations of such collections were made not only by monks but by the Latin clergy: the Roman deacon Pelagius, the sub-deacon John, and the deacon

Paschasius: the clerical order in Rome was interested in the Egyptian spiritual athletes. Benedict had heard of these solitaries while studying as a youth in Rome, and had gone off to imitate them in his cave at Subiaco. When, much later, he wrote his rule for the coenobites of Monte Cassino, he still bade his monks striving for the heights of perfection to ponder their teaching. Not only that, but in the forty-second chapter of the rule he says:

> At all times, when days of fasting or when they eat at midday, if it shall be a day when they thus eat, as soon as they have risen from supper let all sit together and let one read the *Collations* or the *Vitae Patrum* or indeed anything that edifies the hearers . . . or if it be a fast day, when vespers are said, let them go, after a very short interval, to the reading of the *Collations*, as we have said. . . .

The monks at Monte Cassino were, then, familiar with the works of Cassian through hearing him read daily before Compline. Since the RM recommended the reading of edifying books to the monks working in silence, when practicable, it is probable that all monks were fairly familiar with Cassian and the sayings of the desert Fathers; the monks *ad clivum Scauri* and Pope Gregory himself among them. Cassian's teaching and the *Verba Seniorum* were the background teaching also for the Celtic monks whom Augustine's successors were to meet in seventh-century Britain; monks of the Welsh Bangor and of Lindisfarne and southern English minsters had his version of the desert Fathers' teaching in common.

As to the disputed question: how much knowledge of St Benedict was available in Rome when Gregory and Augustine were *ad clivum Scauri*? there was, of course, no 'cult' of St Benedict at Rome, for 'cult' at the time was reverence paid to the body of a martyr, or saint, and it has never been suggested that St Benedict slept at Rome. Yet there is nothing astonishing that the monks at St Andrew's should have heard of St Benedict, for there were many Roman monks interested in contemporary monastic leaders and their manner of practising the *vita monachica*. Valentio, Gregory's abbot of St Andrew's, had been before his appointment a monk of Abbot Equitius in the province of Valeria, and had fled to Rome when the Lombards destroyed his monastery. Gregory selected him to be the first abbot of St Andrew's, and it has been suggested that therefore reverence for Equitius must have exceeded that for other monastic leaders in Gregory's monastery. Yet Gregory recorded from the teaching of Valentio only one miracle of Equitius and, though his reference to Equitius is respectful, he deals with him briefly, in a manner not comparable with the profound reverence he shows to St Benedict, and the length of his tribute to him. It may be that a copy of the RSB was only brought to Rome by refugee monks fleeing after the destruction of Monte Cassino c. 587, when Benedict's disciple, Valentinian, was abbot of one of the small basilican monasteries attached to the Lateran; but there was some connection between these small basilican monasteries and Monte Cassino in Benedict's own lifetime. The basilican monasteries used a form of the divine office familiar to Benedict and anterior to his own (for his adoption of it, see p. 155). It is not impossible that Valentio, like other Roman abbots, had some knowledge of the great monastery of Monte Cassino down on the road to Naples. Gregory, at any rate, says that he learned personally of St Benedict from Constantine (who succeeded him as abbot c. 548 and ruled till c. 560), from the above-mentioned Valentinian, from Simplicius, who ruled after Constantine, and from Vitalis and Bonitus, who were abbots successively; Bonitus was abbot at the time of the destruction of Monte Cassino. If Gregory knew personally all the successors of Benedict, there would seem to have been some contact between the monks of Monte Cassino and Rome.

It has, nevertheless, been argued that Gregory was unacquainted with the RSB from the fact that certain decisions he gave as pope did not follow the specific directions of the RSB. (See Hallinger, *op. cit.* pp. 296–303; Porcel, *San Gregorio,* 1960, pp. 23–35.) This is not the place to go into the matter in detail, but it should be noted that the argument is irrelevant to the question whether Gregory knew the RSB or not. He could not, as pope, have enforced specifically Benedictine usage on monasteries following very diverse forms of the *vita monachica*. He himself, as a member of the clerical order and long before he was pope, was completely free of any monastic obligations. He had to deal with Greek monks settled in Rome; and with Latin monks in Italy, Gaul, North Africa and even Spain; and all these Latin monks followed the general monastic tradition in their own way. To take one point: the variations of Justinian's *Code* and *Novels* in the matter of electing the abbot show that the old manner of selecting the abbot, succession by the senior monk, was giving way to election by the community, and in Gregory's time becoming more general. Succession by seniority, a principle beloved by the Byzantine civil service, avoided disputed elections and had the appearance of justice: but it might easily lead to the succession of an abbot too old for his responsible work, or one who, though very holy, was unfitted to deal with monks by no means perfect (and St Benedict says that monks were often not perfect!) or with the administration of the abbey's possessions. There were similar variations in many other concrete points. Pope Gregory was perfectly free, and showed himself perfectly free, to exercise his own judgment in each case brought before him. But the phraseology of some of his letters and writings certainly echoes some passages of the Benedictine rule.

It is not now held that the monastery of SS Peter and Paul founded by Augustine was a Benedictine house: it must have followed, like the other English minsters, the rule of its abbot: the 'mixed rule'. Yet, since it is very difficult to believe that the RSB was not among the rules studied *ad clivum Scauri*, it would have had its share in Augustine's training. In what respects, therefore, would its teaching have differed from that of the RM and the older rules?

The most important respect would have affected Augustine's training of boy clerics, the children of pagan parents, at Christ Church, Canterbury. This was the insistence in the RSB on the abbot's patience and gentleness in dealing with weak monks. 'It is for us to set up a school of the Lord's service, in instituting which we hope to impose nothing harsh, nothing burdensome.' Benedict's phrases might again and again echo Cassian, but their observances had a long interval between them. Benedict spoke of establishing 'the little rule of a beginning' and half apologised for the lightness of the burden of psalms to be said in the divine office; he allowed a moderate measure of wine at dinner, 'though some say wine is by no means for monks, yet because in our time monks cannot be persuaded to see this, at all events let us agree to this, that we will not drink to satiety but somewhat sparingly'. Benedict emphasised more than once that the abbot must know himself answerable at the judgment seat of God for the souls of all his monks, the bad as well as the good: 'the abbot ought always to remember . . . that to whom more is committed from him is more required; let him know how difficult and arduous a matter he has undertaken, namely to govern souls and to adapt himself to many dispositions. One with gentleness, another with rebukes, another with persuasion, so let him according to the character and intelligence of each monk adapt himself. . . . For the abbot ought to be solicitous with much diligence and to take care, with all sagacity and industry, that not one be lost from among the number of the sheep entrusted to him; for he must know that he has undertaken a cure of weak souls, not a tyranny over strong ones. And let him imitate the good shepherd's example of love, for He, having left upon the mountains ninety-nine sheep, went away to seek one sheep that had strayed.' The abbot's paternal care of the weak in the RSB has no parallel in the RM.

But if the abbot is enjoined in the RSB to exercise a careful, kind and paternal discipline, the monk's obedience is made no less searching. It must be given with good will and cheerfulness, as to the Lord himself: so prompt and alert must a monk be to hear and do the command of a superior in the monastery, that this command and the will of the monk to accomplish it shall be 'mutually enfolded with great swiftness in a single moment'.

Though it is unlikely that the RM should, from its very size, have been among the many books sent by Pope Gregory to Augustine, yet he would have been familiar with the tradition of life in a house monastery which it represents. Nor is it improbable that he should have received the shorter RSB among others for general consultation.

# Appendix 2

### The early form of the vigil and divine office
### and the relation of the Roman-basilican
### office to the Benedictine rule

AUGUSTINE would have been accustomed in his youth to the services of the great Roman basilicas, and in his monastic life to the divine office and eucharist as celebrated *ad clivum Scauri*. Some form of these he would have maintained in his church of the Saviour, certainly without any form of 'popularisation' for his new converts. They would, if they lived near enough and were able, attend the eucharist and such part of the all-night vigil as their zeal or wonder dictated: the form of both was already very old.

The all-night vigil (the παννυχίς, the *vigilia plena*) had been very early celebrated, and with special solemnity for that Sunday which was the anniversary of the Lord's resurrection. For many centuries, and in and after Augustine's time, that day was so observed. Similarly, the all-night vigil was observed on certain other Sundays and feasts, on the night of the great feast of Pentecost, 'as on the night of Easter', when baptism was conferred; on the anniversaries of martyrs, and at Rome on the Sundays after the Ember Days (*Quattuor Temporum*).

Before other Sundays, by the time of Tertullian (*c.* 160–*c.* 240) the vigil was kept, but with a long interval for sleep in the middle. The Christians, he said, meeting for their night assemblies (*nocturnas convocationes*) began the vigil with the evening office (*officium vespertinum*), which they called, from the lighting of the lamps, the *lucernarium* (or *lucernaris hora*); then, at cockcrow, they celebrated the nocturnal office (*officium nocturnum*) and also the dawn office (lauds, or the *officium matutinum*).

Thus, from the breaking up of the all-night vigil, arose the three most ancient and most solemn offices: nocturns (which today are called matins), the matin praises (lauds), and vespers. For some time the general name of the two night offices fluctuated between nocturns and matins; in the second, third and fourth centuries, we hear of the celebration of matins and vespers with mass and agape more often than that of nocturns; matins is commemorated and praised by various writers for particular reasons. Tertullian spoke of the Christians' 'nightly gatherings, if such were appointed', wherein they celebrated the eucharist or the sacrifice of the mass; 'but before and within the sacrifice they instituted prayers, chants, readings and exhortations, which were the elements of the canonical prayer'. Also at the same vespers (vespers as part of the vigil) they assembled 'to take food, casually and harmlessly (*cibum promiscuum et innoxum*)', with prayer of commemoration before and after supper, with lighted lamps and song sung in honour of God 'from holy scripture or composed by themselves'. In these celebrations we have the primitive vespers, agape and lauds: night office, as celebrated before the feasts.

Apparently on other days also the Christians celebrated vespers and the matin prayer; for at such moments, the beginning and end of the day, the religious man spontaneously, as it were, raises up his mind to God, and for the Jewish Christians the times were marked significantly by the morning and evening sacrifice. But the Jewish rite certainly was not the sole or even a strong reason for the Christian vespers and matin prayers, for it is rarely alleged by primitive writers and for a time the new rite of vigil etc. maintained itself in the primitive church rather in opposition to the Jewish rite than as a copy of it; it was the distinctive practice of the Christians. Daily, according to St Cyprian, they said the matin prayers, 'at least privately'.

One description of the vigil prayers comes from the Spanish pilgrim Eucheria (A.D. 385), when she described the various hours of prayer (*horaria*) of the churches in Jerusalem. The description shows a notable difference between the nocturns-matins office of Sunday and of other days.

> Through the week [*per hebdomadam*] the proper office of nocturns was celebrated less solemnly. Before cockcrow all the church doors are then opened in the church of the Resurrection or the Anastasis, and monks and virgins descend, together with certain rather fervent laymen, who wish to keep the very early vigil. And they sing hymns, and psalms are sung antiphonally and antiphons also. And each day there are present two or three

priests who say the prayer after each psalm. But the multitude of
the faithful are absent, as is the bishop and his clergy.

But when it begins to get light, then they begin the matin
'hymns' [or psalms] which seem to be psalms expressly appointed.
Behold now come the bishop and his clergy and at once they enter
into the cave [of the holy sepulchre] and from within the screen is
first said the prayer for all men [this within the office we should
call lauds]. And when the bishop goes out, each man kisses his
hands, and by him they are blessed and dismissed, for now it is
full daylight.

But on the Sunday a huge multitude comes together for the
vigil before cockcrow.

While the church doors remain closed, before the lamps that
are hanging outside, psalms are said and antiphons, and after
each psalm prayers, by the priests or deacons. But immediately
before the first cockcrow [that is, while it is still quite dark], the
bishop approaches the cave and, the doors being opened, the whole
multitude enters the church, where innumerable lights are shining.
There psalms are sung and all make answer, and after each psalm
a priest recites a prayer, and then a deacon recites a prayer, and
then a clerk; and a commemoration is made of all and prayers.
And behold censers are borne into the cave of the Anastasis so
that the whole basilica of the Anastasis is filled with the odour of
the incense. Then the bishop reads in the gospel of the resurrection of the Lord, so that the people are moved to sobs and tears.
And the bishop going out is led with hymns to the chapel of the
Cross and the whole people with him. There again a single psalm
is said and one prayer. Again, he blesses the people and dismisses
them: they go out, kissing the bishop's hands. Afterwards, monks
and certain lay people return to the church of the Anastasis and
they recite psalms and prayers until it becomes daylight.

In this very early description of the vigil office as celebrated
on weekdays and Sundays—the office, that is, after vespers and
before the mass—it is possible to distinguish between the office
celebrated by the monks under the presidency of priests and
deacons, and attended by a few pious lay people if they wished,
in a manner less pre-determined, and the part of the vigil
office really public, celebrated with psalms and hymns in a
manner more pre-determined, by the bishop and all his *familia*

of clergy. To this part of the vigil come the general community
of the faithful. They come in the week to the dawn office which
corresponds to the modern lauds. On Sundays, bishop, clergy
and people attend earlier and celebrate the office with greater
solemnity, with incense and lights.

But this description comes from the east; how far would it
apply to liturgical practice in the west? The evidence shows
that the dawn office, the matin-praises (lauds), was similarly
celebrated in Africa, Spain, Gaul and Italy. St Augustine of
Hippo wrote of his mother that she was wont 'twice a day to go
unfailingly to church . . . that she might hear Thee (O my God)
in thy words and Thou her in her prayers'. St Ambrose exhorted
Christians to hasten in the early morning to church, bringing
the offering of devout prayer. St Hilary wrote similarly. The
monk Cassian was more explicit about the dawn office, which
he called matins, and spoke of as being celebrated in all the
monasteries of Gaul after the psalms and prayers of nocturns
had been said: celebrated after a short interval. 'Finally, in
Italy,' he says, 'today when the matin hymns are finished, the
hundred and fiftieth psalm is sung in all the churches.' He is
clear, that is, that lauds are sung in all the [bishops'] churches
in Italy, not only in monasteries, and that the great *laudate*
psalms are the established ending, before the prayer. There is
other evidence to this effect.

Augustine in his youth at Rome would be accustomed to a
general lay attendance on Sundays at lauds, solemnly celebrated
by bishop and clergy in the Lateran basilica. Priests would
celebrate similarly and apparently with the laity attending, at
the basilica of St Peter, at the Lateran and the other great
basilicas. The mass in secular as well as monastic churches in
the sixth century would be preceded by lauds and attended by
the laity. Psalms 148–50, with which it ended, were described
as a trumpet call (*tuba*), and as the light and joy of an office
appropriate to the hour when light spreads over the sky: the
hour of Christ's rising.

Much has been written about the relation of the ancient
office at Rome to that laid down in the Benedictine rule,
Chapters VIII to XIX. Although by the sixth century the order of
the episcopal office was more or less fixed and ordered, yet the

order was carried out diversely in diverse churches, the order of the Roman church being old and respected, but not known to, and certainly not imposed upon other churches, even those of Italy. The office had certain central points unchangeable at will, and not to be changed by neighbouring or dependent churches; but in the more distant churches even these were unknown. There were, in the language of the sixth century, many different types or *cursus* for the arrangement of psalms, canticles, readings and prayers in the office; the *cursus* of the monks of Egypt or Asia Minor, the *cursus* of Caesarius of Arles (d. 543), the Gallican *cursus* and that of Milan, beside the *cursus* of the great basilicas at Rome, and the Benedictine *cursus*, so minutely desciibed in these chapters of the rule. In Chapter XII St Benedict described the celebrating of lauds for Sundays, and for ferias or week-days when a feast was being kept, in the chapter following. The central or turning points of the night offices, described by St Benedict as nocturns and lauds, are those of the episcopal office of early centuries, as described above.

The *cursus* of the office of St Benedict is of special interest in that we know more about it, from the RSB, than that of any other abbot of the day. There were many abbots in Rome in the days of Benedict, Gregory and Augustine and each was free to order the office as he wished; but it is unlikely that the Roman *cursus* was without influence on any of the Latin monasteries in Rome. We know more, as it happens, about its relation with the RSB.

The familiarity of St Benedict with the Roman basilican office, and his assumption that his monks were familiar with it and that certain features needed no special description in the rule, has been argued and is now generally accepted. In his time not only was the ancient vespers and vigil service celebrated in the papal and other basilicas, but special small monasteries of monks had been established at St Peter's, the Lateran, St Paul's on the road to Ostia, St Mary at the Manger and some other churches. That is, the long office of nocturns, and those of the day hours between mass and vespers, were recited by the monks before the bodies of the apostles or martyrs who slept there. Benedict, as a young man, and many of his monks would have attended the office of lauds, the mass and vespers, with other lay people. He gives no directions for the saying of mass in his rule, assuming that the priest who says it for him will use the order of the Roman church or the church in which he had been trained if he had joined the community after being made a priest. About the office, however, he lays down careful directions.

He says that many 'uses' or *cursus* are flourishing in the different basilicas at Rome. He had lived most of his life in Rome, or near by, and he was educated there. He advises in certain passages of the rule the following of the example of the Roman church, notably in the singing at lauds each day of a different canticle, as the Roman church does. Moreover, he prescribes certain responsories, antiphons and verses whose words he thinks it unnecessary to recite; they must have been well known to those familiar with the Roman use. Indeed, these texts handed down from an ancient traditional use in the Benedictine office agree with those sung in ancient times in the Roman office. Their words are assumed to be known in the Benedictine office.

But this identity of usage by no means extends to the distribution of psalms, which Benedict arranged in his rule with such care and at such length that it seems he was not following an existent use but prescribing his own use or *cursus*. He devotes a whole long chapter (XVIII) to describing 'in what order the psalms are to be said', insisting or even repeating his directions about the order of psalms and even separately for each day hour and the general beginning of the vigil. He indicates the psalms and how they are to be divided; he twice repeats that the vigil for Sunday shall have the psalms from the twentieth onwards, and at length he says that 'if this distribution of psalms displease any man, let him arrange an order he shall judge better'. The whole psalter shall be sung by the monks each week, and on Sundays let a fresh beginning be made at the vigil (*ad vigilias*). (Here St Benedict is using 'vigil' of the nocturn office, now long separated from the *lucernarium* or vesper office.) In all these directions he was not prescribing an order already received.

Indeed, the psalm distribution in the Roman order was quite different in the vigil office and the short day offices; therefore St Benedict indicates the places where his own office differed, while indicating Psalms 148–50 generically under the name *laudes*; these psalms and the daily canticle already had their fixed place in the Roman office, and St Benedict did not wish to change them. They had indeed been universally sung at this office from remote times. Arnobius Junior, a Roman monk who wrote before or about 450 in the City, described Psalm 148 as the trumpet (*tuba*) which at dawn sounded throughout the world.

In one or two other respects St Benedict assumed knowledge of the Roman office, or directly prescribed its usage. He introduced the reading of the short chapter from memory at lauds: the Roman office had no such chapter as late as the twelfth century. But the Roman church had already the short chapter at the little hours (the daylight offices) and here St Benedict followed. Similarly, St Benedict used the expression 'gospel canticle' three times in the rule without further specification; in Chapter XIII, about lauds, it means the Benedictus, and in Chapter XVII, about vespers, it means the Magnificat. The lack of explicit name means that the canticles were in use in the Roman church: that they were in use before Benedict's day.

It has not been proved that the Benedictine rule was among those used by the abbot *ad clivum Scauri* when Augustine was monk and *praepositus* there, or that it was among the books sent for Augustine's guidance by Pope Gregory in 601. The abbot of the Gregorian monastery would in any case have held himself free to order the office himself, and Augustine at Durovernum was similarly free; he had a quite special freedom in arranging the whole liturgy, according to the admonition of Pope Gregory.

But the abbot *ad clivum Scauri*, and Augustine also, must have been acquainted with, if not familiar with, the Roman use in the basilicas; like St Benedict himself, they must have shaped their offices upon it, ordering the recitation of psalms, responsories, chapters and antiphons as they pleased. That Augustine would have celebrated with his clergy and monks, and such laity as cared to attend, the office of vespers, and the old office of the *lucernarium,* at least in the office of Easter Saturday, is certain; his monks would say nocturns or the vigil at cockcrow on Sundays, Augustine attending as and when he could. He, the monks, and the laity, would celebrate the dawn office, on Sundays with lights and incense, and go on to the solemnities of the mass. The day office would be incumbent only on the monks.

# Bibliography

Attenborough, F. L. *Laws of the Earliest English Kings* (1922), for early Kentish laws

Brechter, S. *Die Quellen zur Angelsächsen-mission Gregors des Grossen* (1941)

Chadwick, O. *John Cassian* (1950); for another view, Münz, P. 'John Cassian', in *Jour. of Eccles. Hist.* XI (1960), 1–22

Chavasse, A. *Le sacramentaire gélasien* (1958)

Deanesly, M. *The Pre-Conquest Church in England* (2nd ed. 1963); *Sidelights on the Anglo-Saxon Church* (1962), for Christianity in Roman Britain, and early Celtic Christianity; with Paul Grosjean, 'The Canterbury Edition of the Answers of Pope Gregory I to St Augustine', in *Jour. of Eccles. Hist.* X (1959), 1–49

Dekkers, E. 'Were the Early Monks Liturgical?', in *Collect. Ord. Cist. Ref.* (April–July 1960)

Dix, G. *The Shape of the Liturgy* (1943,) and, more recently, Baumstark, A. *Comparative Liturgy*, Eng. ed. of F. L. Cross (1953), for background of Augustine's celebration of mass at Canterbury

Ewald, P. and Hartmann, L. M. *Gregorii I Papae Registrum epistolarium*, in Mon. Germ. Hist.

Ferrari, G. *Early Roman Monasteries*, Pontif. Instit. of Christ. Archaeology, XIII (Rome 1957)

Frere, Sheppard S., *Roman Canterbury, the City of Durovernum*, (3rd ed. 1962)

Gamber, K. *Wege zür Urgregorianum* (1956)

Grosjean, P. 'La date du Colloque de Whitby' in the *Analecta Bollandiana*, LXVIII (1960); and for an important article on the early dating of Easter, 'La date de Pâques et le Concile de Nicée', in the *Bulletin de la Classe des Sciences*, 5ᵉ Série, XLVIII (1962), of the Académie royale de Belgique

Markus, R. A. 'Chronology of the Gregorian Mission to England', *Jour. of Eccles. Hist.* XIV (1963), 16

Moricca, U. *Gregorii Magni Dialogi Libri IV*, in Fonti per la storia d'Italia, IV (Rome 1924); or, for a more accessible ed. of the *Dialogues*, Pat. Lat. LXXVII

Plummer, C. *Venerabilis Baedae Historiam Ecclesiasticam* . . . 2 vols. (1896), and the Everyman trans. of John Stevenson (1954)

Wormald, F. *The Miniatures in 'the Gospels of St Augustine', Corpus Christi College MS 286* (The Sanders Lectures in Bibliography, publ. 1954)

# INDEX

# Index

*Abbreviations*—ab., abbot; arch., archbishop; bp., bishop; Cant., Canterbury; Co., council; k., king; mon., monastery; p., pope; q., queen; r., river.

Saints are listed under their own names (Benedict, St), but monasteries and churches known by the name of their dedication are listed under St (St Davids, mon.).

Aaron and Julius, SS, 77

Abbot, John, 20, 22; Maurus, 21; of Rimini, 20; duties and power of, 15, 18

*Ad clivum Scauri*, 3, 9, 11; Gregory's foundation on, 13–14, 16, 55, 83, 88, 97, 135, 142, 149, 157

Æthelbald, k., 126

Æthelberht, k., 2, 55, 106; marriage, 24, 30, 108; reign of, 89–91; death, 108; reception of Augustine, 30–4, 39; baptism, 39, 42–3, 59; limits to power of, 46, 83, 112; Gregory's letters to, 50; endowment of church at Cant., 63; Rochester, 74, London, 74

Æthelburga, 111, 131

Æthelfrith, k., 81, 88, 114

Æthelheard, arch., 127

Æthelthryd, 133

Agape, 152

Agapitus, p., 13

Agilberht, bp., 123

Aidan, St, 120, 123

Aix-en-Provence, 24, 26, 28

Alaric II, k., 144

Alban, St, 77, 79

Alchfrid, 123

Alfred the Great, 2, 51

Amfleat, 57

Anchorite, 19; from Bangor, 86–7; Medehamstede, 133

Angers, 29

Angles, northern, 51

Anglo-Saxon Chronicle, 51, 108, 131; Laud version, 132

Anna, k., 119–20

*Apatheia*, 15, 146

*Apothegmata*, 142, 146

Archenfield, 81

Aredius, ab., 135

Arigius, patrician, 28

Arles, metropolitan city and see, 27, 29, 39–40, 42–4, 70–1, 134

Armorica (Brittany), 52, 77

Arnobius Junior, 157

Augustine, St, of Hippo, rule of, 64, 134; and canonical prayers, 154

Augustine, St, arch. of Canterbury, 1–4, 6–24, 100–7; as *praepositus*, 14–20; made bishop, 42; and laws of Kent, 89–92; his *mansio*, 31, 96; his miracles, 73, 85; Gospel book, 98; *Obsecratio Augustini*, 78; 'Augustine's Oak', 82–5, 113; his second meeting with Welsh bishops, 85–7; knowledge of Bened. rule, 135–50; his office at Cant., 157

Aurelian, bp., 19; his rule, 134

Austrasia, 25

Autun, 24, 27, 39

Bamburgh, 123

Bangor, mon., in Flint, 83, 88, 124, 147; learned men from, 85–7

— in Ireland, 113

Banwell, 82

Baptism, Celtic rite, 87; in Kentish churches, 97, 101–3, 109; in Trent, 118

Basil, St, 7–8, 104, 144–6

Bassa, 97

Bede, 2, 23, 26–7, 30, 36, 42, 58; his scholarship, 61, 73, 99–100; his *Eccles. History of the Eng. People*, 2, 60, 62, 68, 77, 84–8, 108; his chronology, 44; *Life of St. Cuthbert*, 62

Belgic tribes, 34; stronghold at Bigbury Wood, 34

Benedict, St, of Monte Cassino, 3, 8, 17, 134–50; relation of his office to that of Roman basilicas, 154–7; his rule, 2–3, 6, 9–10, 13–14, 19, 100, 134–50; cult, 147; successors, 148

— of Aniane, 2, 39, 64, 136

— Biscop, 3, 61–2, 99, 131

Benigne, St, 98

Berhtwald, arch., 58, 112

Bertha, q., 24–5, 43, 49, 50, 53, 79

Birinus, bp., 120

Blaecca, 117

Blood feud, 1, 25
Bobbio, 11
Boniface, St, 68, 125
— IV, p., 110–14
Bot, 1, 90–1, 94
Bradwell (Othona), 97
Breedon-on-the-hill, 133
Brendan, St, 73
*Bretwalda*, 2, 6, 30–3, 42, 45–6, 114; limits to power of, 51–2, 108; lapse of title, 126; relations with Welsh, 83
Bristol Channel, 82
Britain, provinces of, 70; Britains, 71, 76
Brittany, 77, 83, 114
Brixworth, 133
Brunhild, q., 24–6, 39, 47–8, 71
Burgundy, 27–8

Cadoc, St, 83
Caerleon, 79, 82
Caesarius of Arles, 19; his rule, 134
Caldy, 83
Campodunum, 116
Candidus, rector, 23–4, 39
Canon law, 94
Canterbury (Durovernum), 1–7, 11, 24, 30–8, 45–6, 86, 121–2; town plan, 36, 96; as road centre, 97, 130; abbot of, 34, 60; bishop's hall in, 53; burial church in, 55; illumination, 99; learning at, 99; liturgy at, 101–5
Cantware, 36, 38, 44, 52–3, 58, 105
Cassian, 7–8, 81, 100, 135, 145–7; his *Collations*, 146–7; *Institutes*, 146
Cassiodorus, 136, 140–1
Catterick, 116
Ceawlin, k., 51
Celtic: bishops, 46–7, 71, Augustine's policy to, 76–88, 80–8, ordination of, 70, as claustral, 86; clergy, 73, 119; calendar, 119; ornament, 53, 99, 114; scribes, 73; language, 81; laws, 119; Christianity, 76–8, 82–4, 119; Wilfrid and, 131; relations with Rome, 84–8, 112–18; ministers, 128
Cenwalh, k., 82
Cenwulf, k., 127
Ceorl, 90–1
Chad, St, 123–4
Chalon, 29
Charibert, k., 24, 33
Charles the Great, 2, 39, 129
Chelles, 25
Chester, 86; battle, 88
Childebert II, k., 25
Chilperic, k., 25, 47
Christchurch, Cant. (church of the Saviour), 1, 12, 41, 54–5; plan of, 96; life of *familia*, 62, 129
Chrodegang, bp., 39

Church of the Saviour, *see* Christchurch
Clovis, k., 24
Cluny, 6–7
Cnobheresburg, 120
Coifi, 114
Colman, bp., 113, 121–3
Columba, St, 113
Columbanus, monk, 71, 84
Compiègne, 123
Computus, for reckoning Easter, 84, 87–8, 120–2
*Concordia Regularum*, 136
*Confessio*, 54, 75
Congresbury, 82, 120
Constantine I, emp., 10, 43, 50
— II, emp., 77
Constantinople, 4, 11, 16, 135
Conversion of manners, 17
Cornwall, 80
Co. of Aix, 817: 2, 39, 121–2
— Nicaea, 325: 70, 88
— Paris, 614: 57
— Rome, 721: 63
Cross, veneration of, 66, 83
*Cursus*, 155–7
Cutha, 51
Cuthbert, St, 133
Cyneburh, 132
Cyneswith, 132
Cynewulf, k., 126
Cyngar, St, 80, 82, 120

Daniel (Deiniol), St, 83
— bp. of Winchester, 129
David, St (Dewi), 80, 82–3
Deacon, papal, 4, 16, 19, 143, 146; interest in monachism, 146–7; episcopal, 94–5
Deans of mon., 14–15, 19; in RM, 138–9; in RSB, 143
Deda, ab., 118
Deira, 51, 112–18
Denis, St, 56
Desert fathers, 7–8, 11, 19, 83, 104, 119, 134–8, 142
Desiderius, bp., 29, 48
Deusdedit, arch., 112, 123, 132
— notary, 17
*Diaconia*, 8, 10–11
*Dialogues*, of pope Gregory, 3, 135, 142–3
Diocletian, emp., 70
Dionysius Exiguus, 87–8, 121–2
Documents, 16–17; signatures to, 17; at Canterbury, 60–1; *privilegia*, 19
Donatus (Dinoot), St, 85–6
Dover, 30, 86, 97, 130

Eadbald, k., 108–9, 110
Eanbald, arch., 127

Eanflaed, 120
Eanswythe, 130
Earpwald, k., 117
East Angles, 33, 51, 108, 114, 119–20
East Saxons, 34, 51, 58, 60, 108, 110, 124
Eata, bp., 129
*Eccles. Hist. of the Eng. People, see* Bede
Ecgfrith, k., 124
Eddius, 131
Edwin, k., baptism of, 40; his pagan priest, 53; his buildings, 91; death, 97, 118
Egbert, arch., 124, 129
Eorl, 90–1, 105
Eormanric, k., 32, 56, 108
Equitius, ab., 147–8
Eucheria, 152
Eulogios, patriarch, 42–3

Felix, St, 119
Folkstone, 97, 111, 130
Franks, 24–8; traders, 58
Fredegond, q., 25–6, 47
Fursey, St, 120

Galswintha, q., 25
Gaul, Merovingian, 24–30, 48; liturgy in, 65; bishops of, 69–71, 123–4; churches of, 83
Gelasian sacramentary, 66, 102–3
Germanic, ornament, 53, 114; paganism, 89; law, 90, 94
Germanus, bp., 27
Gildas, 77, 80–2
Glastonbury, *see* Yniswitrin
Gloucester, 51
Goodmanham, 53
Gregorian sacramentary, 66, 102–3
Gregory I, p., 1–22; his mission to Anglo-Saxons, 23–30, 115, 127; his sending more helpers, 45–59; his letters, 47, 60–72, 73, 124; use of notaries, 94; altar to, 59; instructions about Celts, 82–3, 87; calendar, 103; sending of relics, 97; writings, 100; books, 102; knowledge of Bened. rule, 135–50
— of Tours, 25
Guntram, k., 25

Hadrian I, 126–7
— ab., 60–1, 78, 85; learning of, 99–100, 133
Hadrian's Wall, 53, 113, 116
Haeddi, bp., 129
Harrow, 34, 105
Hatfield, 115
Helena, St, 83; finding of cross, 85
Hexham, 54, 123, 129

Hilarion, ab., 142, 146
Holy Island, 81
Honorius I, p., 115
— arch., 112, 115–7
Hoo (Hogh), minster, 130, 133
*Husel*, 106, 108
Hygeberht, arch., 126

Ida, k., 81
Ine, k., 94
Iona, mon., 112, 120–1
Irish Channel, 76–7, 81
Ithamar, bp., 132

Jænberht, arch., 126
James the deacon, 113, 118
Jarrow, mon., 60, 62; learning at, 99–100
Jaruman, bp., 132
Jerome, St, 31, 100; and desert Fathers, 146–7
John, bp., 22
— of Réomé, 134
Justinian, emp., 144; his *Code*, 144–9; *Novels*, 149
Justus, arch., 45, 58, 109; ordination of, 70, 75; recalled to Durobrevis, 110–11; death, 117

Lateran, basilica of the Saviour, 10; its basilican monasteries, 10, 18; office, 154–5
*Laura*, 138
*Lausiac History*, 141–2
Lawrence, St, 79
— arch., 18, 42, 57–8, 99, 108–10; mission to Rome, 44–8; bearer of letters, 62
Lector, 17
Leo III, p., 127
Leonine sacramentary, 102–3
Lérins, 11, 24, 26, 29, 83, 119; under mixed rule, 134, 142
Lichfield, 125–7
Licinius, bp., 47
Lincoln (Lindum), 117
Lindisfarne, 62, 115, 123, 147; gospels, 99
Liturgy (eucharist), 102–6; monastic liturgy and offices, 104, 138–40; Augustine's query, 65–6; Gallican rite, 66
Liuthard, bp., 30, 37, 39, 55, 79
Llandaff, 80, 82
Llansannam, 80
Llantwit, 80, 83
Lombards, 4–5, 11, 56, 147
London (Londinium), as a port, 60; as a see, 40, 45, 49, 74, 86, 109–10
Lothar I, k., 24
— II, k., 25, 47

Lubin, ab., 134
*Lucernaria*, 138, 151, 157
Lullingstone, 77
Lupus, bp., 47
Lympne (Limynge), 38, 97, 131
Lymynge, *see* Lympne
Lyons, 27–9

Makarios, St (the elder), 134, 137, 142–6; (the other, or the younger), 137
Marriage: degrees of, 62, 67–9
Marseilles, port, 24; province, 28
Martin, St, of Tours, 36
Martyrium, 77–80; possibly at Canterbury, 78–80
Maserfield, 120
Mass, 96, at Cant., 100–3; early eucharist, 152–4
Maurice, emp., 49
Maximianus, ab., 16
Medehamstede (Peterborough), 131–3
Medway, r., 74, 111
Melantius, bp., 48
Mellitus, arch., 45–9; bishop of London, 58, 109–11; ordination of, 70
Mercia, 2, 118, 120, 125–7
Metz, 25, 28, 39
Minster in Sheppey, 130–1
— Thanet, 131
Mixed rule, 3, 42, 128–33
Monasticism, Benedictine, 2, 135, 138–150; basilican mons., 10, 21, 155; oblates, 23–4; monastic tonsure, 5–6; early monasticism, 6–13, 134–150; child oblates, 139; Greek monasticism, 10, 12; Syrian and Armenian, 76; minsters in Kent, 130–1, in north, 131, in Mercia, 131–2
Montserrat, 3
Moot, 90–1
Mund, 91

Neustria, 25, 47, 60
Ninian, St, 113
Northumbria, 51–3, 81–2, 118, 124
Notary, 16, 23, 32, 94–5
Nothelm, arch., 27, 31, 68; his journey to Jarrow, 60–1

Octa, k., 32
Odo, arch., 54
Offa, k., 77, 126–7
Oisc, k., 32
*Opus dei*, 18–21, 128, 140, 144; nocturns, 151–3; matins, 151–3; vespers 151; lauds psalms, 154, 157
Orleans, 25

Oswald, k., 120, 126
Oswiu, k., 113, 121–4, 126, 132

Pachomius, 7–8, 104, 144
Padarn, St, 83
Panuthios, ab., 137
*Paradisus Heraclidis*, 141
Paris, 24, 33, 56, 123
Partney, mon., 118
Paul the first hermit, 146
Paulinus, arch., 40, 45, 112–18, 120, 131
Peada, k., 118, 123; founds Medehamstede, 132
Pelagius, deacon, 19
Penda, k., 52, 116, 118–19, 132
Persecutions: Valerianic, 79, Diocletianic, 70
Peter the Apostle, 50, Petrine see, 121–2; dedication to, 132
Peter, papal deacon, 143
Peter the monk, 44, 57, 62
Petroc, St, 82
Picts, 53, 113
*Praepositus*, 8, 13–18, 39, 131; in early rules, 137–9; St Benedict's use of, 143
Protasius, bp., 28

Quartodecimans, 122
Quentavic, 29

Rædwald, k., 33, 114, 117
Rector in Campania, 20, in Gaul, 22
Reculver (Regulbium), 38, 97
*Responsiones* of pope Gregory, 61–3; contents, 63–72; two forms of, 62
Rhone, r., 24, 27
Richborough, 38, 97
Ricula, q., 34, 51
Ripon, 129
Rochester (Durobrevis), 58, 74, 100, 109–12, 130
Roman law, 1, 16–17, 58, 69, 94–5
Romanus, bp., 111
Rome, early mons., 12–16, early nunneries, 12; pilgrimage to, 83
Rouen, 29
Rufinianus, ab., 45
Rufinus of Aquileia, 146
Rule of the Master, 6, 9–11, 19, 64, 100, 129, 134, 150; authorship of, 140–2

Saeberht, k., 34, 58, 108
St Andrew cata Barbara, mon., 12
St Andrew, church at Rochester, 58, 74
St Aristus, mon., 12
St Davids, mon., 124
SS John and Paul, mon. at Vatican, 12

St Martin, church of, Cant., 36–8, 79, 96; baptisms at, 40–1
St Mary at the Manger, 10, 155
St Pancras, mon. at Lateran, 10, 80, 97; church at Cant., 96–7
St Paul, basilica of, on road to Ostia, 10; mon. at, 12, 57, 155
St Paul, church in London, 58, 74
St Peter, basilica of, on Vatican, 10, 57, 98; office at, 154–7
SS Peter and Paul, Cant. mon., 3, 42, 57–8, 75, 96–9, 110, 149; services at, 103; mixed rule at, 149
St Peter, church of, Cant., 37
St Saba, mon., 13
St Sebastian, church of, 10
St Stephen, mon. at Lateran, 10
St Stephen by St Lawrence, mon., 12
Salisbury, 82
Samson, St, 82–3
Saviour, church of, Cant., 36, 38, 41, 83
*Scopa*, 32
*Scrinium*, 23–4, 40, 47, 62; Nothelm's visit to, 60–1; Boniface writes to, 68
Seaxwulf, bp., 131–3
*Secundus* in mon., 15, 19–20
Sens, 29
Serapion, ab., 137
Serenus, bp., 47
Severin, St, 79
Severn, r., 82
Severus, emp., 70
Sigeberht, k. of East Angles, 119–20
Sigebert, k. of Franks, 24–5
Silchester, 37, 54, 77
Simplicius, bp., 47
Sixtus II, pope, 72; 'the martyr Sixtus', 78–80
Sledda, k., 51
Soissons, 25
Somerset, 51, 81
South Saxons, 51, 60
Stephen, ab., 29
Stipends, at Cant., 63
Stour, r., 30, 38, 43, 118
Sutton Hoo, 53, 117
Syagrius, bp., 27, 29, 39
Synod, govt. by, 95; ?703 Aetswinapath, 131; 746 Clofeshoh, 124, 126; 747 in north and south, 126–7; 803 Clofeshoh, 127

Tatwine, arch., 112
Teilo, St, 83
Tertullian, 152
Thames, r., 74; Roman bridge over, 74
Thanet, 30
Theft, penalties in Anglo-Saxon England, 67, 94
Theodebert (Thibert), 26–8

Theodore, arch., 58, 61, 88, 94, 112, 124–5; learning under, 99–100
Theodoric (Thierry), k., 26, 48
Thor, 1, 53, 57, 89, 105
Toulon-sur-Arroux, 47
Tours, 24, 83; mon., 119
Trier, 40; capital of Gaul, 70; martyrium, 79
Tuda, bp., 123, 132
Tynemouth, 81, 113

Valentinian, ab., 148
Valentio, ab., 14, 147–8
Vegetius, 114
*Verba Seniorum*, 145, 147
Vergilius, bp., 29, 39
Verulam, 79
Vienne, 29
Vigils, 41, 96, 103–5, early forms of, 151–4; before Pentecost, 43, 151, before Easter, 66, 151, before Christmas, 72, before Ember Days, 151; Bened. form, 156
*Vitae patrum*, 19, 147
Vitalian, p., 121, 125
Vivarium, 135, 141
Vosges, 71

Wantsum, 30, 34
Watling Street, 36, 38, 75, 86, 97, 110, 131
Welsh, 52, 80
Wer, 1, in Kent, 90–1
Wessex, 2, 95, 109
West Saxons, 33, 51
Whitby, synod of, 84, 87, 113, 118, 121–2
Wighard, 125
Wilfrid, St, 54, 113, 121–4, 129, 131–2
Wimbledon, 51
Winchester, Old Minster, 95
Wine, bp., 124, 132
Wing, 54
Witan, 94–5, 114
Wite, 1
Woden, 1, 32, 53, 105
Wulfhere, k., 124
Wulfric, ab., 98
Wulfstan, arch., 95
Wynfrith, bp., 131

Xenodochium, 30, 42

Yeavering, 53, 91, 116
Yniswitrin (Glastonbury), 82, 96, 120
York (Eboracum), 40, 46–9, 116, 123–4, 132; baptism of Edwin, 114

Zacharias, p., 125